I0416013

Shackled: Why We Are Predisposed to Resist Belief Change and How to Overcome Our Instincts

Fiona So

Published by Fiona So, 2023.

SHACKLED: WHY WE ARE PREDISPOSED TO RESIST BELIEF CHANGE AND HOW TO OVERCOME OUR INSTINCTS

Second edition. January 19, 2024.

Copyright © 2023 Fiona So.

ISBN: 978-1-304-69114-9

Imprint: Lulu.com

Written by Fiona So.

Table of Contents

Foreword

Throughout history, we have seen time and again that revolutionary ideas often face resistance, even when they hold the potential to save lives or alter our understanding of the world. Consider the tale of a Hungarian physician in the 19th century.

The Story of Ignaz Semmelweis: The Savior of Mothers

In the not-so-distant past, childbirth was a dangerous procedure. Before the 20th century, the maternal mortality rate could reach as high as 10%[1]. This means that 1 in 10 mothers could die during childbirth. What was supposed to be a joyous occasion was often overshadowed by the tragic loss of life. Determined to solve this problem, a Hungarian physician in the 19th century began investigating the matter, hoping he could find something to save mothers and their families.

He observed that mothers in the hospital where he worked were much more likely, compared to mothers who gave birth at home, to develop puerperal fever. Following this clue, he had a daring hypothesis: he suggested that the infection might actually be introduced to the mothers by the doctors. At the time, doctors often used corpses for medical training and research. The physician proposed that the infection might be carried from the dead bodies to the mothers by the doctors themselves.

Keen to test his theory, the physician proposed a new policy mandating all medical staff to wash their hands with a chlorinated lime solution before examining mothers. At first, this was met with skepticism and resistance because doctors at the time believed diseases were caused by "bad air" (miasma), so the appropriate measure should have been fumigating places or spraying perfumes and aromatics to cover bad smells. Plus, accepting his theory would mean that doctors were responsible for the deaths of those mothers.

Despite the pushback, the physician persisted. In the end, the superiors relented and let him implement this new practice. To everyone's surprise, ever since the new mandate took effect, the mortality rate had dropped significantly to just less than 2%[2].

One might have assumed that such an achievement would be recognized as a triumph, deserving of the physician's inclusion in the Hall of Fame. However, reality proved to be quite different. Despite the policy's evident impact, the physician's superiors and colleagues persisted in rejecting his theory. They derided him for his supposed stroke of luck and dismissed his ideas as pure coincidence. The physician endeavored to gather evidence to support his case, only to have it disregarded by academics as the physician could not articulate the underlying reason why his hand-washing policy could reduce the mortality rate (Keep in mind that they didn't have any knowledge about germs or bacteria back then).

Deeply frustrated and upset by the lack of acceptance of his idea and proof, he became increasingly difficult to work with. Eventually, he was driven out of the hospital. But the physician didn't give up on his discovery. After leaving the hospital, he returned to Budapest and continued his struggle in his hometown. He continued advocating for proper sanitation and handwashing through articles and lectures. Unfortunately, despite compelling evidence, he remained largely ignored because he still could not provide a theory to explain why his practice was successful. Coupled with his confrontational personality, he became the subject of ridicule and rejection again.

Eventually, the stress and anxiety took a toll on his mental well-being. In 1865, he was committed to a mental asylum where he did not receive proper treatment. When he was committed, the physician was restrained in a straitjacket, imprisoned in a dark cell, and severely beaten by several guards. Soon after, he passed away due to blood poisoning, which developed from his infected wounds.

Meanwhile, the hospital he had worked at had abolished the practice of hand sanitizing after the physician's resignation. Although the maternal mortality rate returned to the previous level, everyone chose to ignore this apparent correlation between hand-washing and maternal mortality. Why should they anyway? After all, the Miasma Theory was the dominant theory and there was nothing about hand sanitizing.

That was the story of Ignaz Semmelweis, who was posthumously called the "Savior of Mothers." It was unfortunate that he did not have enough time to witness the day when his theory was vindicated, as it took a few more decades and major breakthroughs to happen. Shortly after his death, Louis Pasteur, the father of microbiology, began procuring microscopic evidence that helped add credibility to the Germ Theory. Later, Robert Koch also conducted an experiment on anthrax that contributed to the traction of Germ Theory. Their experiments both supported the wider acceptance of the correlation between germs and disease, and more scientists performed experiments confirming the theory. Nonetheless, it was only in the 20th century that Germ Theory could replace Miasma Theory as the dominant theory in the medical field[3].

The Human Tendency to Resist Change

Apparently, the acceptance of new theories can be a lengthy process, even in the presence of compelling evidence. *Something about us just makes us stubborn and resistant to changes.* Often, significant hardship is required before any meaningful progress on the acceptance of new theories can be achieved. What happened to Ignaz was unfortunately not an exception. History is filled with a litany of examples where people fought against the dogma. Take the Father of Modern Physics, Galileo Galilei, as an example, he proposed that the Earth orbited the sun, contradicting the Catholic Church. As a result, Galileo was declared a heretic and placed under house arrest. Rachel Carson, the Mother of the Environmental Movement, documented the harm caused by pesticides in Silent Spring, yet she faced accusations of being "hysterical" and a communist who was trying to undermine American agriculture. Ada Lovelace, one of the first computer programmers, endured constant skepticism and challenges just because computing was seen as a man's field.

It'd have been great if our literacy and education could help us be more open minded, but the truth is, *we are no less stubborn today*. There is an extensive list of discoveries from the past decades, or even centuries that are still being rejected today. Take global warming as an example; it was first discovered in the 1970s, yet some deny human impacts despite the ironclad evidence, claiming that it is a conspiracy theory co-created by the government and renewable energy businesses. I've begun to think that we might actually cross the Point of No Return in 2030[4] when it becomes impossible to reverse the damages, we've inflicted on Planet Earth. Another pertinent example is vaccination. Over the past 200 years, the efficacy and safety of vaccines have been well-established. Nevertheless, there are still those who believe that vaccines can cause autism and infertility. Consequently, we are witnessing the resurgence of diseases like measles and polio in regions where they were once on the brink of eradication.

The Challenge of Overcoming Cognitive Biases

Why do beliefs persist despite contradicting evidence? The answers we have thus far are simple: humans are flawed; we are biased, and our judgments can be irrational. While numerous suggestions have been proposed by philosophers and academics to address biases, several key questions remain unanswered:

- What causes our biases? Are they innate or learned through experience?

- If biases are rooted in our nature, can we genuinely overcome them, or are we destined to be influenced by them forever?

- How can we navigate the challenge of making informed decisions when we are predisposed to cognitive biases?

- Is it possible to reconcile opposing beliefs, finding common ground, and fostering understanding despite the presence of biases?

These questions are the reasons I started writing this book. Drawing from neuroscience, psychology, and philosophy, I explore the origin and impact of cognitive biases, specifically belief resistance and confirmation bias. The first half of the book examines the mechanisms behind our decision-making processes, uncovering the factors that shape our beliefs and the challenges we face when those beliefs are challenged. But this book is not merely about understanding biases; it is about empowering you to transcend them. Armed with knowledge and insight, we will navigate strategies for overcoming these cognitive pitfalls in the second half of the book. We will uncover techniques for making more informed, objective decisions, fostering effective communication, and embracing a mindset of growth and adaptability.

Embarking on a Journey of Self-awareness and Growth

Change is not easy - it requires us to confront our own biases, challenge our long-held beliefs, and open ourselves to new possibilities. Yet, as history has shown, these transformative leaps are essential for progress. From the pioneering minds of Ignaz Semmelweis to the trailblazing efforts of Galileo Galilei and Rachel Carson, we will draw inspiration from those who dared to challenge the status quo, despite facing resistance and ridicule.

As you embark on this journey, I encourage you to approach these pages with an open mind and a willingness to question your own assumptions. Embrace the opportunity to reflect on your own biases, explore new perspectives, and develop strategies for navigating the complexities of decision-making. The road ahead may not always be easy, but the rewards of self-awareness, growth, and improved decision-making await those who venture forth. *Not all of us have to be pioneers of change, but at least we can be supporters rather than blockers of improvement.*

Here, I also want to express my heartfelt gratitude to those who have supported and influenced this book, from mentors and colleagues to friends and readers. Your contributions have shaped and enriched this work, and I am grateful for your presence on this journey.

Now, without further ado, I invite you to turn the page and embark on a transformative exploration of the mind. Let us challenge our biases, embrace new possibilities, and unlock the untapped potential within ourselves. Together, we will navigate the intricacies of perception, overcome our cognitive biases, and embark on a path of personal growth and meaningful change.

Chapter 1 - The Bayesian Brain

———

We have always known that humans are imperfect beings. Throughout history, there have been countless instances where humanity has faltered and failed to learn from its past mistakes. Despite our shortcomings, we still managed to become the master of the planet Earth for we have inherited the most powerful gift from evolution: Intelligence.

Without any guides, our Stone Age ancestors knew how to use resources like fire, stones, and animal skins to overcome environmental challenges and increase their chances of survival. They understood the importance of documentation, learning, and communication, leading to the invention of languages. This allowed us to collaborate and pass down knowledge to future generations. The accumulation of knowledge provided us with a significant advantage over other animals. Gradually, we unraveled nature's mysteries, gaining control over our surroundings. We've become capable of devising proactive and ingenious solutions that anticipate and preempt problems. For instance, our ancestors pioneered the practice of agriculture for a more efficient means of obtaining food, revolutionizing our ability to ensure a stable food supply. Recognizing the risks associated with relying solely on fire for illumination, we invented the lightbulb, offering safe and reliable light. Additionally, in response to the growing need for land to accommodate expanding populations, we undertook ambitious projects like land reclamation and mountain reshaping. *As a species, we possess a unique capacity to transcend mere adaptation, actively shaping the environment according to our will.*

Neuroscience 101

While some animals get deadly venoms and sharp claws, we get something much more powerful: the neocortex. This is the outer layer of the human brain responsible for higher cognitive functions, such as perceptions, language, reasoning, and planning. The neocortex is 76% of our brain[5], and humans have the largest neocortex in relation to brain size amongst all animals[6]. This difference sets us apart from all other animals.

The reason why size is important here is because of the primary composite of the neocortex: neurons. Neurons are the fundamental building blocks of the brain. By connecting with one another, they form numerous intricate networks to transmit electrical and chemical messages with different parts of the body, giving rise to thoughts, speeches, perceptions, and movements in response to external stimuli. They can also encode memories in the neural pathways. Therefore, the more neurons we have, the more computational power and storage we get.

To illustrate how the firing of neurons and formation of neural pathways give rise to intelligence, let's consider a simple example. In kindergarten, teachers introduce new vocabulary words to students. For instance, let's focus on the word "apple." The teacher presents an image of an apple, spells out the word, and pronounces it. Through visual and auditory stimuli, the students associate the image, word, and sound, forming a neural pathway that encodes this information. Later, when the teacher shows an actual apple, the neural pathway related to "apple" is activated, enabling the students to recall and pronounce the word. *The ability to translate external stimuli into biochemical signals and encode information explains why we have the ability to learn.*

While this example simplifies the complex interplay within the brain, it demonstrates the *general process of learning*. We can encode not only objects but also experiences and observations. We constantly refer to our prior knowledge and experience to make predictions about future events. For instance, let's consider a scenario where we were burned by a boiling tea kettle during our childhood. In addition to triggering pain signals that prompt an immediate withdrawal and a cry for help, our brain also encodes this experience and establishes a neural pathway associating the tea kettle, heat, and pain. Armed with this prior experience, when we encounter a tea kettle in the future, we can then predict the possibility of being burned. This is where the interesting part comes in. We make use of what we've learned to predict what comes next, and our prediction of what comes next determines our actions now. Circling back to the tea kettle example, in order not to get burnt the second time, we'd now approach it with caution. *Our ability to learn and predict is the reason why we are capable of exceptional problem-solving and prevention skills for we're the only species that can learn, adapt, and anticipate.*

The Bayesian Brain

Now, what if this is a different tea kettle that looks nothing alike from the previous one, would we still be able to recognize it and approach it with caution? The answer is obviously a yes, but let's talk about how. When our brain encodes information, we encode attributes[7] of a tea kettle, i.e. the spout, the handle, and the lid, rather than just that specific tea kettle itself. The next time we see a tea kettle, even though it's of different color, material, or even design, we'd look at the attributes of this object and generate the most probable explanation of what this is based on what we know. Strictly speaking, we don't necessarily "know" that it's a tea kettle; it's an *educated guess* based on what we know about tea kettles before. *Our brain takes the most probable guess based on prior knowledge and what it is currently receiving as sensory stimuli and this guess will become the basis of our perceptions. It becomes our reality, and therefore, the basis of our reactions and decisions.* In this particular scenario, we'd still approach this possible tea kettle with caution, so we won't get burned.

This applies not only to object recognition but also to abstract concepts and experiences. Let's take the concept of trust as an example. Through our interactions and observations, we develop a general understanding of what trust entails, including aspects such as reliability, honesty, and dependability. When encountering a new individual or situation, our brain can analyze the attributes and patterns present and generate an assessment of trustworthiness based on our prior knowledge and experience.

However, there is an inherent challenge in this mechanism. We don't possess knowledge of all possible scenarios, nor do we have the precise probabilities associated with each outcome. This raises the question: *If we lack complete information, can the probabilities we assign ever be truly accurate?*

This brings us to a thought experiment[8] introduced by English statistician Thomas Bayes. He wanted to know the probability of the first ball he threw landing on the right side of the table. For us, this would have been a wild guess, but Bayes wanted to raise the confidence level of his guess. So, after having thrown the first ball, he asked his assistant to drop a second ball and report whether it landed to the left or right of the first ball. The idea is simple: if the second ball is to the left of the first ball, it's more likely that the first ball is on the right side of the table. He then repeated the process, with Bayes *updating his answer based on new information until he reached a high level of confidence in his guess.*

Legend has it that this thought experiment gave rise to the Bayes Theorem, a fundamental concept in mathematics and statistics that uses prior probability to calculate the probability of an event occurring under specific conditions, and as the prior probability changes, the posterior probability would also change accordingly. That way, even though we don't have knowledge of the entire population, we can still refine the confidence of our guess. *That, surprisingly, is also how our brain generates perception.* It incorporates our prior belief and incoming stimuli to give us the most probable explanation of our surroundings.

To illustrate this, let's consider an example. Imagine you're walking in a park and spot an animal in the distance. Based on past experience, it's more likely that you will see dogs in this park. Therefore, you initially assume that the animal you see is likely a dog. That is our *prior belief*. As you observe the animal more closely—taking note of its size, shape, color, and behavior—you evaluate the confidence of your initial guess. If the new sensory information aligns with your initial hypothesis, you become more convinced that it is indeed a dog. Conversely, if the new information contradicts your initial assumption, you start considering alternative possibilities. *As you gather more information by approaching the animal, you refine your initial hypothesis to align with reality as closely as possible.*

What Does This Tell Us About Being Human?

This phenomenon is known as the Bayesian Brain Hypothesis, a theoretical framework in cognitive neuroscience that explains how we form perceptions and make decisions based on both prior beliefs and incoming sensory information[9]. In essence, it suggests that our perception is not a direct representation of the external environment, but rather a subjective interpretation based on our unique experiences. While this mechanism seems simple, its implications are profound, and it explains the imperfections of humanity.

One significant implication is that it provides a biological basis for the *inevitability of disagreement*. Although we are aware of this phenomenon, we often expect others, particularly those close to us, to perceive the world as we do. When disagreements arise, we tend to overlook our differences and may even blame others for being irrational or idiotic if their viewpoints don't align with our own. This was evident during the massive protests in my hometown, Hong Kong, in 2019. The city became permanently divided into two camps—yellow ribbons (anti-government) and blue ribbons (pro-government). These opposing sides held contrasting views on every topic, from police brutality to extradition laws and the appointment of Chief Executives. Unfortunately, people on both sides found it impossible to empathize with each other. Tensions escalated to the point where derogatory language and insults were used, such as calling each other "cockroaches" or "yellow objects," further deepening the divide. Eventually, many people publicly renounced relationships with their friends, partners, and even family members. Regrettably, I was one of those. I stopped contacting my relatives for almost 3 years because of our divide in this protest.

If only we recognized that our perceptions and decision-making are shaped by our own unique experiences, and if only we acknowledged that we are inherently wired to have different perspectives, would we have responded with greater compassion and patience?

Probably not, because the other significant implication from the Bayesian Brain Hypothesis is the *inevitability of cognitive biases*. By default, we approach issues and individuals with initial assumptions based on our prior experiences and knowledge, regardless of their accuracy.

But does this mean we are forever bound by our biases? Doesn't the Bayesian Brain Hypothesis provide us with a mechanism for updating our beliefs in the face of new information? In theory, starting with biased interpretations doesn't mean we have to remain stuck in those biases. However, the reality is different. History is filled with examples of individuals refusing to change their minds even when confronted with compelling evidence. Galileo faced persecution and was placed under house arrest, Ignaz Semmelweis wasn't recognized as the Savior of Mothers until after his death, and Rachel Carson was vilified as a communist. These instances demonstrate our resistance to change.

So, what hinders the update mechanism? Now that we've established the basis of how perception is formed and decision is made, the following chapters will explore the forces that block the update in our beliefs. We will examine various historical examples that illustrate our biases—how we selectively attend to information that confirms our hypotheses, reject alternatives that contradict our beliefs, and deny change despite compelling evidence. Throughout this exploration, we will also delve into the biological mechanisms that hinder the update process in our brains, as well as strategies to reactivate it.

Chapter 2 - Our Battles Against the Grip of Fear and Our Past

On March 3, 1913, a day before the inauguration of President Woodrow Wilson, a stream of women marched down the streets, waving colorful banners and flags[10]. However, don't be mistaken; they were not celebrating the impending inauguration of the President. Instead, they were participating in one of the most significant parades for women's suffrage back then, a parade that would eventually change the course of history.

The parade featured approximately 8,000 women from diverse regions. Some participants wore costumes representing their backgrounds, while many others dressed in the suffragist colors of white, purple, and gold, symbolizing purity, steadfastness, and hope. They marched in well-organized groups, proudly carrying banners, signs, and flags adorned with powerful slogans such as "Votes for Women," "Equal Suffrage," and "We Demand an Amendment to the Constitution." Elaborately decorated floats showcased scenes depicting women's significant contributions to society, while symbols of justice and equality were prominently displayed. Adding to the spectacle, marching bands provided rhythmic melodies and music, encouraging the marchers to sing along as they paraded through the streets. The lively and captivating nature of the parade attracted thousands of spectators, who eagerly witnessed this historic event.

However, not all spectators embraced the parade. While it went down in history as one of the most powerful and liberating scenes, the majority of people found the parade offensive, immoral, and treacherous. Women's suffrage was a highly contested issue during that time, facing strong opposition from many men, including politicians and religious leaders. Politicians argued that women lacked the intelligence and rational thinking necessary for political participation. Religious leaders viewed women's involvement in politics as a blatant violation of divine rules, citing religious texts that portrayed women solely as wives and mothers.

Surprisingly, opposition to women's rights was not limited to the male gender. In 1911, American educator Josephine Dodge founded the National Association Opposed to Woman Suffrage[11]. This organization played a significant role in opposing the women's suffrage movement. They published various forms of literature, including pamphlets, books, and articles, to voice their opposition. They organized their own rallies and actively lobbied politicians to ensure that proposed amendments granting women's suffrage would not pass. Prior to the parade, tensions were already built up between the two sides through many rounds of public debate.

Returning to the scene of the parade, some spectators started hurling insults and obscenities at the suffragists as they marched. Others resorted to more aggressive actions, throwing rotten vegetables, stones, and even firecrackers, hoping to intimidate and disperse the marchers. However, despite these attacks, the marchers remained steadfast and undeterred. In response, the anti-suffragists decided to escalate their actions. Tens of thousands of them flooded the streets, blocking the parade route. Confrontations turned increasingly hostile. Some anti-suffragists spat on the marchers, while others attempted to forcibly remove the suffragists from the parade. These escalating actions eventually culminated in direct physical assaults. By the end of the day, over 100 women had sustained injuries and required hospitalization[12]. To compound the injustice, the police, who held sympathies for the anti-suffragists, unjustly blamed the women for endangering themselves by attending the parade. In a disappointing turn of events, the anti-suffragists faced no consequences for their actions.

The Night of Terror

While the violent actions of both the anti-suffragists and the police incited public outcry, such violence was not an isolated incident in the history of the women's right movement. Four years later, in 1917, Alice Paul, the organizer of the 1913 Parade, decided to stage another impactful event before President Woodrow Wilson's second term. This time, rather than a large parade, she opted for picketing[13]. Regardless of the weather, suffragists would gather, donning distinctive purple, white, and gold sashes, and holding signs that boldly stated, "Mr. President, how long must we wait for liberty?"Unfortunately, even in this peaceful act of protest, the suffragists faced taunting and assault from anti-suffragists. While they sat quietly, holding their signs, they were subjected to harassment. To compound the injustice, the police joined in, issuing tickets to charge the protestors with traffic obstructions. Over time, the penalties escalated from fines to prison sentences. On November 14, 1917, 33 women suffragists were imprisoned at Occoquan[14]. The prison's superintendent, William H. Whittaker, called upon his guards to "teach the suffragists a lesson," and the guards carried out his orders with enthusiasm. They dragged the women down the stairs to a dark, filthy cell and subjected them to worm-ridden food. Some suffragists were ruthlessly thrown onto an iron bed, rendering them unconscious. One particularly unfortunate suffragist had her arms twisted and banged against an iron bench. When news of these atrocities surfaced, the media referred to the event as the Night of Terror. It stands as one of the most egregious abuses inflicted upon suffragists in the history of the movement.

The Seed of Aggression

Reflecting upon the anti-suffragists' brutal behavior on the Night of Terror, one might ask: Were these individuals inherently violent or evil? Could such atrocities stem from hatred simply because we disagreed with each other? There's a saying that the smallest dogs often bark the loudest. In this context, the aggression exhibited by the anti-suffragists was not necessarily driven by an inherent penchant for violence or malevolence. Instead, it could be seen as a *manifestation of fear—fear of losing their ability to comprehend the world*, should their long-held beliefs about women's roles in society be challenged.

As discussed in the previous chapter, our mental models are continuously shaped by our experiences and learnings, enabling us to interpret the world around us. However, not all assumptions within these models hold equal weight. Some assumptions are not pertinent to explaining the ways of the world and are expected to evolve over time. One example would be fashion choice. No one would start a war just because now people prefer to wear yoga pants instead of jeans. *However, some assumptions are the foundation of how society works, and those are generally not expected to change drastically, or at all.* Gender roles is an example that falls into this category. For thousands of years, women were predominantly perceived as mothers and nurturers within the family unit. Their sphere of influence was primarily domestic, leading to the notion that they need not concern themselves with educational or career pursuits since men would provide for them. Given their role in maintaining households and caring for children, the idea of women needing property ownership rights or the right to vote seemed unnecessary. Although this perspective is now considered highly inappropriate and sexist in the present era, it was the prevailing consensus for many societies over the course of millennia. Even in Ancient Greece and Rome, known for their democratic systems, women were typically excluded from public life and political participation.

When a norm has withstood the trials of time, we seldom question it or give it much thought anymore. It would just be taken as the *foundational truth governing the ways of life*. Consequently, when someone challenges this norm and asserts its inaccuracy, irrelevance, or injustice, it can feel as though a fundamental building block of society has been removed. Suddenly, everything appears unstable and uncertain because we can no longer interpret our surroundings, let alone interact with and respond to them. This incapacity to predict and devise responses is one of our greatest fears as humans, as we rely on these abilities to control our surroundings. *Changes, no matter how justified, mean we must relinquish our control, at least temporarily, and who can predict what might happen then?* The chairman of the National Association Opposed to Woman Suffrage encapsulated this sentiment well when she rejected the idea of women's suffrage, stating it was "unwise to risk the good we already have for the evil which *may* occur." While challenges to our prior beliefs may not physically harm us, our brains perceive them as *threats*, triggering the amygdala and putting us on a *warpath*.

Amygdala and Our Fight or Flight Response

The amygdala, a small almond-shaped structure in our brain, functions as a security guard. It constantly scans for potential threats that could harm us, both physically and mentally. When it detects a threat, it triggers a series of biochemical responses, resulting in the release of stress hormones such as cortisol and adrenaline. These hormones enter our bloodstream, initiating a cascade of reactions in the body that prepare us for the well-known "fight or flight" response. Our heart rate increases, breathing quickens, and blood flow is redirected from non-essential organs, like the stomach, to our extremities. *These physiological changes not only affect our physical state but also alter our priorities.* We become solely focused on survival and self-preservation. Consequently, our brain simplifies matters into two categories: threat or not-a-threat. We become hyper-focused on potential threats while ignoring other stimuli. Our predictions also become biased, with an increased perception of the likelihood of something negative happening.

Now that you're immersed in this heightened state, a choice presents itself. You can either confront and neutralize the perceived threat, or you can opt to withdraw from the situation. However, there's no time to deliberate. In the case of the anti-suffragists, seeing that they had an advantage in numbers, it was possible that their brains jumped to the most straightforward option, and that was to overpower the suffragists. Other considerations such as consequences and moral implications of their actions were deprioritized. Before they knew it, they were already hurling insults and objects at the marchers, hoping to intimidate them into abandoning the campaign. None of these stemmed from malevolence, but rather, a desire to protect themselves from the need to adapt to an unknown.

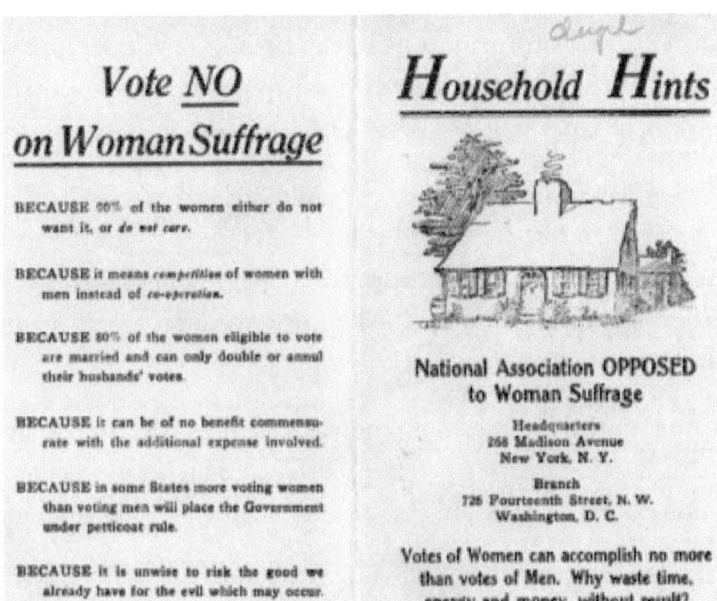

Household hints pamphlet distributed by the National Association Opposed to Woman Suffrage (NAOWS). circa 1910[15]

Old Habits Die Hard

Regardless of where the violence stemmed from, the acts of anti-suffragists were nonetheless heinous. However, please note that the mobs only represent a fraction of the populace, and not everyone resorts to violence when facing fear. While the violent group maybe unapproachable, would the nonviolent group be more open minded? The answer is not as straightforward as it might seem. Just because the nonviolent bunch doesn't throw stuff at you doesn't mean they are more likely to change their minds when confronted with contradictory information. While our brains have the capacity to learn new things and update existing beliefs, this doesn't mean they easily shift perspectives, even in the absence of fear.

While the brain does possess the ability to learn and adapt, in order to abandon our prior beliefs and integrate with the new one, we have to build and reconstruct our neural pathways and this process can take time - it is simply impossible for us to just take in new beliefs right away.

As mentioned before, our knowledge and prior beliefs are encoded in our existing neural pathways. To increase efficiency, neural pathways that are constantly activated would upgrade to fortify their connections[16]. Gradually, more dendrites and receptors would grow to enhance signal transmission efficiency. Some may even develop a myelin sheath wrapping, which acts as an insulation coating to minimize signal loss. *This mechanism is the reason why practice can lead to mastery.* Take language as an example, we don't really have to think about the words when we speak in our mother tongue, something that we speak every day. Athletes are another great example, by virtue of the hours they put in their practices, their movements and reactions have become reflexive. The fortification of connections can greatly reduce our cognitive load while increasing efficiency. The best thing is that the fortified connections are less susceptible to decay. Let's say you've emigrated to another country for a couple of years now and you rarely get the chance to communicate in your mother tongue, though you may get a little rusty, you'd still remember the language.

When we apply this general mechanism to deeply ingrained beliefs and ideologies that we take as foundational truth to our worldview, it's likely that these pathways are *fortified*. Therefore, it'd *require a longer period of inactivation to dismantle these old pathways.* For example, if you have held religious beliefs for many years, it would likely take time to transition to atheism and vice versa. The same principle applies to the concept of gender roles. It is unlikely that an anti-suffragist would suddenly become receptive to the idea of gender equality, as their existing neural pathways associated with their beliefs are already fully developed and fortified, making their ingrained concepts, however outdated, much more accessible.

The Necessary Evil

That leads us to an unfortunate conclusion: *our biological designs predispose us to be biased against change.* We are biologically incapable of just abandoning beliefs, particularly when they're deeply rooted, and we are wired to caution against changes as we see uncertainty as threats. While the challenges associated with our predisposition have been extensively discussed, it's also important to consider the benefits and the necessity of belief resistance. *Fear has an evolutionary advantage*; it prompts us to think more deeply about the issue. When we harness the power of fear, it allows us to be more prepared and preempt problems before they even happen.

Stickiness of our neural connections is also very crucial. By not immediately changing our beliefs when confronted with new information that contradicts our prior beliefs, we ensure the *efficient and timely construction of a coherent reality*. This approach enables us to interpret and navigate the complexities of the world without overwhelming cognitive overload. It allows us to respond effectively to the rapid changes in our surroundings, making our daily lives more manageable.

The Best of Both Worlds

The ancient Greek philosopher Aristotle once stated that virtue lies in finding a balance between excess and deficiency in various aspects of life[17]. This applies to the issue of resistance to change as well. On one hand, being too receptive to new ideas may suggest gullibility and fickleness. On the other hand, completely dismissing anything that contradicts our prior beliefs implies stubbornness and close-mindedness. Thus, it's important to *strike a balance and aim for the best of both worlds*.

Instead of concerning ourselves with "the evil which may occur", we can see uncertainty and change as an opportunity to improve. *At the end of the day, we are where we are now because we've made a lot of changes in the past.* Instead of believing in absolutism and the divine power of Kings, we now believe in democracy and constitutionalism. Instead of trialing people with ordeals of fires, we now have a judiciary process to examine evidence before giving out verdicts. Instead of letting the market to freely determine the price, governments would now intervene and provide a baseline protection to the citizens through minimum wages, etc. All of these were once vehemently opposed due to their potential to disrupt the status quo, but history has shown that these changes have contributed to a *more compassionate and just society.*

I encourage everyone to remember the positive outcomes that change can bring. By incorporating these positive examples into our existing beliefs, our Bayesian brains may become less apprehensive and pessimistic about the uncertainty that change brings. By keeping our amygdala in check, we will have the mental space to challenge our fears and validate our assumptions, gaining a deeper understanding of whether our concerns will be realized. Gradually, as we go along with the journey of change, we may be able to *turn our apprehension into hope.* When we see the benefits of the changes, it'd be easier for us to alter our neural pathways and integrate with the new changes, because reward is just as powerful a driving force as fear, which we'd discuss more in the next chapter.

The ability to regulate our apprehensions against our fears and stay open minded is becoming more important now than ever. We live in tumultuous times; while we grapple with leftover issues from the 20th century, we are now faced with a new list of challenges, including climate change, political polarization, and a widening income gap. The frustration of people suggests that the established orders of the 20th century no longer fit the needs and trends of the current era, and frustration is the catalyst for change. We see more campaigns and protests than ever, signaling a period of major changes. Instead of resisting change in the name of stability and caution, I urge you to reflect on your own beliefs and attitudes toward change.

Embrace changes as an ally and actively contribute to shaping this transformative journey peacefully.

Chapter 3 - The Hidden Cost in Our Pursuit of Pleasure

In the previous chapter, we explored the underlying factors behind belief resistance, namely the *persistence of thoughts and the influence of fear*. When we encounter new beliefs that contradict our existing ones, it can be extremely challenging for us to immediately change our minds. Moreover, our fear of change compels us to resist any form of transformation, often at any cost. In some cases, this urge becomes so overwhelming that it can turn a peaceful individual into an aggressive mobster, resorting to violence. When fear permeates a crowd, the inclination towards violence can rapidly escalate from verbal insults to physical assaults, and even to large-scale warfare.

Fear, with its ability to limit our openness to new experiences and inhibit discovery, learning, and progression, is one of the first emotions studied in neuroscience and continues to receive significant attention. But fear is just one of many elements that block us from improvement. On the other end of the emotional spectrum, there's a more insidious force that can trap us in our own reality: the sense of pleasure.

Like fear, pleasure also garners a lot of attention but for completely different reasons. We want to know what helps us reduce our own fear, but above all, we want to know what makes us happy. After all, that's what life is about, isn't it?

Happy Hormones Assembled

Here's what we know so far: unlike fear, the experience of pleasure is a lot more complicated as it involves multiple neurotransmitters and brain systems working together. This suite of neurotransmitters includes endorphins, serotonin, oxytocin, and GABA[18]. Each of these neurotransmitters has a slightly different impact. For example, endorphins are often associated with pain relief and satisfaction, and when overproduced, they can even result in euphoria. Serotonin, on the other hand, contributes to feelings of happiness and contentment, providing the foundation for self-confidence. Oxytocin, also known as the "love hormone" or "cuddle hormone," is associated with feelings of security that stem from trust, closeness, and belonging. Finally, GABA is an inhibitory neurotransmitter that promotes a sense of calmness and relaxation, providing the foundation for a general sense of well-being.

Regardless of these nuanced differences, our brain generally labels these as positive emotions that we crave. So, whenever we experience these positive emotions, our brain records the experience and the triggers associated with it, so we can recognize what makes us happy.

At this point, I'd like to introduce a special member of the suite of "happy hormones[19]". This member, dopamine, doesn't directly contribute to the sense of pleasure per se, but it plays a very important role in the reward mechanism.

Dopamine: the Fuel that Carries Us to Our Goals

While dopamine is often perceived as a pleasure molecule, it's more accurate to categorize it as a "motivation molecule". Contrary to common belief, the mere release of dopamine doesn't induce a feeling of pleasure. Instead, dopamine is released in anticipation of pleasure, propelling us towards actions that promise rewards[20].

When we expect a reward (i.e., things that have triggered positive feelings before), we experience a spike in dopamine. This spike prompts motivation, creating an urge in us to go after the reward we desire. For example, let's say you really enjoy desserts and you've just walked past a café with a whole cabinet of cakes on display. At this moment, you recognize the rewarding stimuli (i.e., the cakes), and your brain triggers the release of dopamine. Your eyes sparkle and you pause in your tracks. The next thing you know, you're at the shop making a purchase. When you finally have the cake you desired, you feel a sense of joy and dopamine is released again to reinforce this behavior. As a result, the next time you walk past a cake shop, it's very likely that you will repeat the act, anticipating the same joy.

The Pursuit of Confirmation

So, how does this dopamine release link to confirmation bias? Dopamine, a neurotransmitter integral to the brain's reward system, incentivizes actions leading to anticipated rewards. *When the reward we seek is the satisfaction of believing we've gained understanding or unraveled mysteries, dopamine propels us to continue seeking information that confirms our initial assumptions*[21]. This inclination can lead us to selectively disregard contradictory information and interpret ambiguous or irrelevant information in a way that supports our pre-existing beliefs.

Collectively, these behaviors constitute the infamous confirmation bias. It's infamous because it can skew our perception. But that's not the worst part. As you cherry-pick information and biasedly interpret ambiguous information to support your view, it's likely that you will draw a conclusion with "reasons" (however biased or untrue) that confirm your prior beliefs. When you do, dopamine is released again to reinforce your initial belief. Through reinforcement, the pathway experiences the upgrades that I've mentioned earlier. It becomes more efficient, more accessible, and more lasting. *This last step completes the reinforcement cycle.* Not only are we wired to warp our perceptions to validate our prior beliefs, but we're also predisposed to reinforce our beliefs on a neurological basis using the distorted reality we create for ourselves. This leads to an unfortunate conclusion: *it's very likely that we are unwittingly trapped in a feedback loop that leads us further and further away from the truth.*

When Justice Gone Astray

Although this feedback loop doesn't directly trigger aggressive behavior like fear does, its impact is no less detrimental. While fear leads us to reject change, this feedback loop can lead us to fervently create our own reality that ignores information from the actual reality. When this distorted reality becomes the basis of our judgments and reactions, we can unknowingly hurt innocent people. In some circumstances, we can even ruin the life of an innocent person.

In 1992, a 28-year-old man was convicted of 2nd-degree murder and was sentenced to 25 years of imprisonment for a murder he didn't commit. This unfortunate man was Frank Sterling. He was implicated in the murder of a 74-year-old lady, Viola Manville[22]. In 1988, she was brutally murdered while taking her daily walk. The lady was shot twice in the head with a BB gun, struck with a railroad tie, and beaten to death. When the body was found, she was also stripped naked from the waist down and her jacket was pulled up with her breasts exposed.

This gruesome, cold-blooded murder caught the attention of the public, and police were pressured to solve the case quickly. They quickly identified a list of suspects, one of which was Frank Sterling. Although Frank didn't have any prior criminal records, he was targeted because his brother, Glenn Sterling, had been sent to prison for attempted sexual assault on Viola Manville before. The working theory was that Frank abused and murdered Viola to avenge his brother, and it was the most promising story at the time. However, Frank was dismissed from the investigation after all because he had an airtight alibi - he was working at the time of the murder and his coworkers testified for him. When the most promising lead was proven invalid, the investigation didn't progress. The case had turned into a cold case.

In 1991, a new investigation team was formed to revisit this high-profile murder. He flipped through the file and looked at all the evidence collected from the crime scene. The tire tracks matched the type of car that Frank's sister was driving. The fiber collected was also the type of clothes that Frank usually wore. As far as evidence goes, these were merely circumstantial. But all of this provided hope to the investigator at the time. Perhaps the alibi was not true, he thought. Perhaps Frank was just really good at covering up his tracks.

So, they visited the eyewitness again with the picture of Frank and asked if she had seen Frank at the scene of the crime back in 1988. Although the eyewitness back then denied having seen Frank, this time, she confirmed it. The investigator felt he was closer to solving the case than ever. He could practically confirm that Frank was the murderer. It's just that the evidence on hand and the testimony wasn't good enough for court. He needed something more - a confession.

The police invited Frank to the police station. Although Frank had just finished a 36-hour shift, he complied with the request. Throughout the interrogation, Frank was asked about details from 3 years ago. Naturally, he didn't have much recollection (Do you remember what said or did a month ago? I don't.), but the police saw this as Frank being dodgy. The police then started pulling out the photos and key case details, claiming that these were prompts to help Frank remember what he did.

But Frank insisted on his innocence.

No matter, the police weren't listening. Seeing that he didn't "admit to his crime", the police then shifted tactics[23]. They had Frank lay on the floor with his feet up and his eyes closed, telling him that it was okay for Frank to admit what he had done, and that it was totally understandable that he would want to avenge his brother and unleash his anger on the victim. Throughout this time, Frank kept emphasizing his innocence, but the police didn't listen. They kept coming back with different tactics to suggest that he was the murderer.

This interrogation lasted for 8 hours. By then, Frank had been awake for almost 2 days. Unable to endure such interrogation any longer, he cracked and admitted he did it. The police pulled out the camera and taped a confession from Frank. As Frank was exhausted, the police had to keep reminding him what he should be saying, and Frank basically just repeated after the police. It wasn't the best confession, but the police got what they needed. Despite the objection from Sterling's attorney on the validity of the tape and Frank's immediate recantation, the judge admitted it as evidence and Frank was convicted of second-degree murder.

Although he was eventually exonerated in 2010, he had already spent 18 years in jail for a crime he didn't commit. Can you imagine spending 18 years in jail for something you didn't do? Can you picture a reality where no one believes you and no one wants to hear your side of the story? What happened to Frank was certainly an atrocity. While we would like to think of this as an unfortunate exception, the reality is it happens more frequently than we imagine. According to the National

Registry of Exoneration[24], up to October 19, 2023, there have been 3399 wrongful convictions since 1989, and more than 30,250 years were lost. To put things into perspective, 30,250 years is almost *three times as long as the entire recorded history of civilization.* These are just numbers of people who were lucky enough to be exonerated in one country - the United States. Who knows how many more wrongful convictions there are in the whole world?

Social Media: The Digitized Reward Mechanism

Wrongful conviction is obviously one of the topics of focus; and I'd like to believe that the criminal justice system of certain countries is undergoing improvement, however slowly, by raising the burden of proof and adopting forensic technology to refine accuracy of accusations. While these are all great measures to lower the possibility of wrongful convictions, I hate to say that it would still be impossible to reach zero wrongful conviction. No matter how high the burden of proof, how precise the technology is, we are still predisposed to confirmation bias. Process and technology can only do so much. At the end of the day, we are the ones making the inferences and drawing the conclusions based on the available data points, and the most insidious thing about confirmation bias is that it affects our interpretation. *Instead of solely relying on external guardrails to reduce confirmation bias, we must raise awareness ourselves.* We need to be wary of our own urge and tendency to cling onto the first instinct we have.

This awareness is particularly important with the current design of social media. We are in the age of information. As we demand access to a vast amount of real-time information, we are blissfully unaware of the trade-off on accuracy. Everything we see now is fragments of the truth. We see titles that seem to have concisely summarized the issue but left out the context. We see pictures that seem to have accurately captured the essence of what happened but again, left out the prequels that built up to the moment of the image. We see articles that are hastily written from just one perspective and left out the rest. Worst of all, we reward the media, however innocuously, for providing us with these fragments because they satiate our need to have some answers about what's happening. We give our reactions based on the first glance of the picture. We express our thoughts right away after seeing the title. We share and repost these posts to perpetuate the spread of these fragments. Knowing what plucked our heartstrings, the social media continued to feed us similar information that confirmed our prior beliefs so they could keep getting engagement from us[25]. In a way, social media is a digitized version of the reward mechanism.

As we bask in the joy of being know-it-alls, we must recognize the potential harm we can inadvertently cause. Innocent lives can be wrongly accused and vilified due to snap judgments fueled by confirmation bias. In 2001, a biodefense researcher was wrongfully accused of being the culprit of an anthrax attack just because he had the means to access the bioweapon. It took him seven years to clear his name and settle the intense media scrutiny[26]. In 2010, Christopher Jefferies faced public vilification because the media portrayed him as the killer of his tenant due to his eccentric appearance[27]. In 2013, Sunil Tripathi went from a missing person to the culprit behind the Boston Marathon Bombing because a user compared his photo with the grainy photo of a suspect released by the FBI, and the post went viral[28]. For these victims, they didn't suffer from wrongful conviction, but simply *wrongful accusations are enough* to ruin their reputations and wreak havoc on their lives.

We Are Our Own Guardrails

To prevent the perpetuation of such tragedies, it is crucial for us to recognize the power of confirmation bias and be vigilant about our own thought processes. We must take steps to break free from its grip. One effective measure is to verify the accuracy of information before accepting it as truth. Seek out reputable sources and cross-reference multiple reports on the same issues to gain a comprehensive understanding of different perspectives.

Additionally, it is essential to actively seek out sources that contradict our own opinions. Just because something challenges our beliefs does not mean it is worthless or irrational. We need to acknowledge the possibility that we might be wrong and be open to hearing diverse viewpoints. By actively engaging with differing perspectives, we foster intellectual humility, patience, and resilience.

These practices are crucial for establishing a solid groundwork of comprehensive and adaptable opinions. They allow us to reassess and update our beliefs based on new evidence and information, freeing ourselves from the limitations of confirmation bias. Through actively seeking reliable sources and embracing diverse perspectives, we empower ourselves to make better-informed decisions and make meaningful contributions to a society that values inclusivity and balance. I believe that the advantages of making quality decisions can activate the same reward mechanism, but with a shift in focus. Rather than reinforcing cognitive biases, it encourages a deliberate and thoughtful thinking process. By knowing how our mind works, we can always turn our weakness into strengths and foster a more robust decision-making approach.

Chapter 4 - Bending Reality: The Role of Cognitive Dissonance in Shaping Beliefs

---

So far, we've discussed how we're predisposed to be biased against changes and how we're motivated to confirm our belief. While they are different issues, the mitigations are similar - one of which is to deliberately expose ourselves to thoughts and information that contradicts our beliefs, training ourselves to be more open-minded. However, this is easier said than done. We are predisposed to seek consistency and whenever there are contradictions between our prior beliefs and new information, then we would undoubtedly experience a sense of discomfort and tension.

This is a psychological phenomenon known as cognitive dissonance. *It is the discomforting psychological state triggered by any inconsistency between thoughts, beliefs, or actions*[29]. The stress would then motivate us to reduce or resolve the dissonance by either changing their beliefs or modifying our behaviors. However, we've already talked about how we simply cannot change our beliefs overnight because it takes time to dismantle the neural pathways. Moreover, we *may not even want to change* our beliefs because of both the power of fear and reward. Our urgency to free ourselves from such discomfort then leads us to rationalize and justify the inconsistency however we can, a technique called *rationalization*[30].

Cognitive Dissonance in Action

Let's look at procrastination, a classic example of cognitive dissonance that arises due to inconsistency between our own goals and behaviors. We all know that work needs to be done and there's a deadline to our assigned tasks. However, the world is filled with temptations. We can spend hours scrolling through social media, devoting the day to leveling up our characters in games, or enjoying a good nap. After succumbing to such temptations, we're filled with a sense of discomfort and unease because our behavior is not aligned with our beliefs and objectives. To ease our discomfort, we can start picking up the work that awaits. However, most of us probably would justify procrastination by telling ourselves that we work better when the deadline approaches. After all, work is stressful, and procrastination is fun.

Now, let's take another example of cognitive dissonance when we encounter new information that challenges our prior beliefs. Let's say you're a strong believer in freedom of speech, but then you can't help but notice a surge in online hate speech. In some instances, victims have even chosen to commit suicide because they couldn't take the cyberbullying anymore. You can't help but wonder if a certain extent of content moderation is needed, but this control mechanism contradicts your belief in free speech.

Now, there's a choice to make. You can simply resolve the inconsistency by choosing one of the two directions to pursue and abandoning the other. You could acknowledge the problem with hate speech and accept a certain degree of content moderation. But again, we are predisposed to resist belief change. A much more viable alternative at the time is to create a plausible explanation to reconcile the contradictions. For instance, you could acknowledge the presence of hate speech but dismiss it as an outlier and an exceptional case that no one should take any actions on. You could also downplay the impact of hate speech by saying that these are just words, and the victims shouldn't take them to heart. Along the same line of thought, you could even state that hate speech encourages open dialogue and exchanges, however offensive and hurtful they may be.

As flimsy and invalid these arguments may be, as long as they *make enough sense to us*, they can reconcile the contradictions and *resolve the sense of unease and discomfort*. It's the *fastest* way for us to break free from the state of discomfort, without having to spend the cognitive effort to revise our beliefs while enjoying the sense of validation by thinking that we are still right. So, it doesn't matter if those arguments are completely invalid, the most important thing to our brain is that we are happy, that we are not confused or drained.

While we have already discussed the power of fear and anticipations and how they can distort perceptions and judgments, neither is nearly as powerful as rationalization driven by cognitive dissonance in its ability to bend the truth. In some extreme cases, it can even create a parallel universe that's completely delusional.

The Undying Theory: Zetetic Astronomy

One such example is the Zetetic Astronomy, more commonly known as the Flat Earth Theory. For most of history, even before we had the ability to venture into space, we've always known that the Earth is a sphere. However, in the 19th century, an English inventor and writer, Samuel Rowbotham, decided to conduct experiments to challenge this scientific consensus. He waded into the Old Bedford River and set a boat with a flag 3 feet above the water to row away from him[31]. The experiment was simple. If the Earth is a sphere, then there should be a curvature, and the flag should have disappeared from his sight as it rowed away. However, that wasn't his observation at all. The flag remained in sight for the full six miles, and so he drew the conclusion that the Earth was flat. He then published a book called Zetetic Astronomy: Earth Not a Globe, which gained popularity for a short while. Lots of people tried to replicate the experiments, but it was quickly debunked by another scientist - Alfred Russel Wallace[32]. He dispelled the flat Earth Theory by including considerations for atmospheric refraction, which then explained why Samuel could see the boat even with curvature around the Earth. The Flat Earth Theory was officially discredited.

But the Pandora's box had been opened, and there was no turning back. Even though Rowbotham's work had been invalidated, it is continually cited by proponents of the Flat Earth Theory. Curiously, one would have thought that this theory would die out after we've ventured into space, but that wasn't the case at all. Over the years, more and more people believed in flat Earth and contributed to the theory. And nowadays, an estimated 2% of Americans believe that the Earth is flat[33]. But it's not just America, there are chapters of flat earth societies all around the world. Every year, there is an International Flat Earth Convention for these believers to meet up, share their passion for this belief, and seek consolation from each other.

For years, the Flat Earth Theory and its believers have been a media sensation. What is so special about this theory that would attract people from all over the world to believe despite being repeatedly discredited by the scientific community? How could it withstand the challenges from the photographic evidence that we could now obtain from space?

Shape of the Earth: a Globe or a Flat Disc?

Whilst Flat Earthers may come from different ethnicities and backgrounds, they all share a common trait: deep distrust against the government and NASA[34], and the root of such distrust might have been inadvertently contributed by the most significant milestones of human civilization: the moon landing back in 1969.

For the first time in human history, humans had the ability to venture outside our home planet. Even if it was just a short trip to the moon, everyone was very excited at the prospect of space travel. The launch was televised, and everyone celebrated the success of the launch. In 1972, when the astronauts returned, they were met with the warmest welcome. Everyone wanted to learn more about their experience, and the astronauts had done a number of tasks on the moon. They collected rock and soil samples from the lunar surface and brought them back to the Earth for scientific analysis. They deployed a range of scientific instruments and experiments on the lunar surface, such as laser retroreflectors, which enables precise distance measurements between the Earth and the Moon. They've also taken extensive photographs and films to record their activities on the Moon, including the images of the lunar landscape, and the experiments they've conducted. One of the most famous photographs was the insertion of the American flag on the lunar soil. The act, as well as the photo, was symbolic - it represented the first successful voyage of humans into space. It symbolizes the success of decades of work from numerous people. It was evidence of a dream come true.

Apollo 11 astronaut Aldrin saluting the flag at Tranquility Base[35].

Sadly, not everybody felt the same. Some started scrutinizing the photo and noticed some abnormalities that they couldn't understand. In the photo, the American flag appeared to ripple or move as if there was wind, despite the Moon having no atmosphere. One thing led to another, people started to raise questions on the lighting and shadows on the photos and footage, as if there were multiple light sources. In an attempt to reconcile the existence of these official footages and photographs and the oddities they couldn't quite explain, they have created the Moon Landing Hoax and suggested that the entire moon landing was staged by the government filmed in a television studio.

For some, this marks the beginning of the distrust of NASA and the U.S. Government. They have started to wonder what else could NASA have lied about if NASA could fake the moon landing? During the mission, there was another famous photo taken by the astronauts, and it was the Blue Marble, which was an iconic photograph of the Earth that is still frequently used nowadays. Conspiracy theorists suggested that this photo was also faked as it was edited (Just to be clear, the edit is to add contrast and brightness only, not to change the shape). For those who were exposed to Flat Earth Theory before, the suspicion had just crossed the threshold from just the moon landing to the shape of the Earth.

Blue Marble – Image of the Earth from Apollo 17[36]

Eager to confirm their suspicion, some Flat Earthers started looking for more information about the shape of the Earth. The religious ones would refer to ancient religious texts, which ambiguous wordings were interpreted by them as "evidence" that suggested a flat earth. The others recreated the Bedford River Experiments and fashioned some new experiments, such as the Laser experiments and the Airplane "level flight" experiments, which they'd record and share their results on social media, championing the Flat Earth Theory.

To counter their campaign effort, the scientific community responded. There were a number of videos from scientists and Globe Earthers debunking the misunderstandings of the Flat Earthers by introducing concepts such as principles of aerodynamics and atmospheric refractions. But this supplementary information was not well received by the Flat Earthers; instead, they saw it as an attack on their belief, and that sentiment was the last push that forever separated the two camps. They have gradually widened their scope of scientific theories that they'd reject to maintain the consistency of the Flat Earth Theory, and this list includes the concept of gravity, distances of the sun and moon, size of the solar system, and size of the planetary bodies etc. Gradually, their theory is describing a completely different universe that operates under a completely different set of laws. What started as a suspicion has now turned into a theory that becomes the bedrock of reality for the believers.

When the Belief Has Become Impenetrable

Some scientists were curious at the significance of the divergence and decided to approach the Flat Earthers in person. The hope was to understand their perspective, where the ideas came from, and hopefully instill some scientific knowledge to dispel their misconceptions. However, the accounts always had the same feedback - that rational conversations with the Flat Earthers were practically *impossible*[37].

In case you are wondering exactly how *impossible* the conversation could be, I invite you to hop on YouTube and see for yourself. There is a YouTube channel called Jubilee and in one of their videos, they invited three scientists and three Flat Earthers to discuss the shape of the Earth[38]. While all six of them went into the discussion in good spirits, the debate got so intense midway that the director had to press pause and distribute bottles of cold water to help everyone calm down. Not only did the Flat Earthers reject everything that the scientists said, but they also branded themselves as the truth seekers who were free from manipulation by the mainstream media, and that the other side for being misinformed and uneducated. *When a belief is integrated with one's identity, it becomes impenetrable*[39]. Whatever contradictory evidence presented would be disregarded and countered right away, and there is no room for discussion, let alone compromise. Despite the effort to regulate the intensity of the discussion, the theoretical physicist was visibly frustrated towards the end of the video, while the other two scientists regularly exasperated and sighed.

In the comment section, lots of people expressed sympathy towards the scientists as they had to put up a discussion with "ignorant, uneducated" people. The general sentiment is that it is impossible to win an argument against "fools". One of the comments has captured the essence of the sentiment with a quote from the former German Chancellor, Helmut Schmidt: "Arguing with idiots is like playing chess with a pigeon. You can be the best player in the world, but the pigeon would still knock all pieces over, poop on the board and go out in triumph".

While these comments pin the problems to the intelligence of the Flat Earthers, we need to understand that *cognitive dissonance and rationalization can bend the reality of even the best thinkers in history*. One of the examples was the father of modern philosophy - René Descartes.

The Irrational Arguments from the Most Rational Man on Earth

René Descartes was a polymath. Not only was he a philosopher, but he was also a scientist and a mathematician. In science, he was studying the fields of optics and proposed the laws of reflections (which was refined later). In mathematics, he invented the Cartesian Coordinate System, which laid the foundation for analytical geometry, and the integration between algebra and geometry was a groundbreaking development in mathematics. But his most reputable achievements were in the field of philosophy. He was a prominent figure in promoting rationalism, which was an ideology that emphasized the power of human reasoning as the primary means of acquiring knowledge. Rationalism aside, he also created a methodological approach, known as the Cartesian Skepticism, that emphasized skepticism and doubt as a means to arrive at certain knowledge. He was so radical in his skepticism that he reexamined everything and boiled down to one irrefutable, foundational truth - "Cogito, ergo sum", which translates to one of the most famous quotes nowadays - "I think, therefore I am".

With his achievements and contributions to science, René Descartes was surely a man of logic and rationality. However, not all of his arguments were equally valid and sound. In his arguments on the existence of God, he received a lot of criticism from various philosophers. Let's take a look at the argument[40]. He posited that he had this idea of a perfect, all-powerful being (God) in his mind. Given he was such an imperfect and limited human, he couldn't have come up with such an idea on his own, so he concluded that his idea must have come from a being that actually possesses those perfect equalities. Simply put, his conclusion was that the idea of a perfect God must have been caused by a perfect God.

I believe this should sound strange even to the non-philosophers among us. Why must something exist for an idea to happen? There are no wizards in the world but nonetheless J.K. Rowling created a whole wizarding world in her books. There are no intergalactic travels but nonetheless

George Lucas invented the world of Star Wars. Clearly, things don't have to exist for an idea to happen.

For a person who advocated rationalism and skepticism all his life, it was surprising that he couldn't see the flaws in this particular argument. Before we judge him too harshly, we should understand the background of the father of modern philosophy. René Descartes was actually a devout Catholic for his entire life. His family was Catholic, and he was educated at the Jesuit Collège Royal Henri-Lé-Grand in La Flèche, which was known for its strong Catholic teaching and rigorous intellectual program[41]. Throughout his life, Descartes maintained a strong connection to his Catholic faith, and his religious beliefs played a significant role in shaping his world view.

For Descartes, the physical world was seen as a creation of God, and his curiosity about the natural world stemmed from his desire to understand God's divine plan. He believed that by unraveling the mysteries of the natural world, he could gain a deeper understanding of God and His work. Descartes saw science as a means to comprehend the intricacies of creation and approach a better understanding of God[42].

However, as Descartes delved deeper into the realms of science and philosophy, he likely encountered conflicts between his religious beliefs and his rational, philosophical inquiries. The challenge of reconciling his identity as a scientist and philosopher—a seeker of reason—with his identity as a believer—a person of faith—could have led Descartes to grapple with cognitive dissonance and engage in rationalization. This is a common human tendency, as *changing deeply held beliefs can be difficult, especially when they are intertwined with one's sense of self.*

Navigating Cognitive Dissonance in Conversations

René Descartes' story serves as a powerful reminder that *our inclination towards cognitive dissonance is not necessarily linked to intelligence.* As humans, we are wired to resist changing our beliefs, particularly when those beliefs are integral to our identity. We instinctively strive to safeguard our worldview from being shattered. This behavior is not a measure of intelligence but rather a reflection of our innate resistance to belief change.

When engaging with individuals who exhibit cognitive dissonance, it is crucial to approach such discussions with empathy and understanding. It is all too easy to dismiss others as ignorant or unintelligent, but holding such an attitude only fosters defensiveness and reinforces their commitment to their beliefs. This phenomenon is known as the *backfire effect*, a cognitive bias that occurs when people become more entrenched in their original belief despite contradictory evidence[43]. Unfortunately, this often leads to greater polarization of opinions.

Therefore, it is important to recognize our inherent predisposition to cognitive dissonance. By acknowledging this, we can cultivate open-mindedness, empathy, and engage in thoughtful dialogues that transcend the limitations imposed by our deeply held beliefs. Instead of perpetuating the backfire effect, we should strive to foster an environment of mutual respect and understanding, where differing perspectives can be explored and discussed constructively.

Logic 101

A conversation goes both ways. While empathy and understanding are encouraged, we certainly can't take others' patience and compassion for granted. Therefore, I call for all of us to work on the quality of our thoughts so as to overcome our tendency to justify our resistance to belief change. Like all problem-solving frameworks, we must first be able to detect the problems. In the context of overcoming biases, we should then regularly *check the quality of our arguments* behind our decisions.

To assess the quality of an argument, we can look at the *soundness* and the *validity* of the argument. *Soundness refers to the truthfulness and accuracy* of the premise, and the best way to ensure soundness is to look at the evidence. We've already covered some tips in ensuring accuracy of information in the previous chapter so here, I'd mainly focus on the other element: validity of an argument. Assessing the validity of the argument can be tricky because our inferences are subject to bias. To help us with that, we can park some of the frequently used logic rules in our pocket.

Let's start with the easiest: Modus Ponens. It says that if "A implies B", and "A is true", then "B must be true". So far so good, right?

Now let's try to add a little bit of complexity by doing a backward inference. While "A implies" B is still true, now you're given another fact that "B is true". Do we know if A is also true?

Most people would probably reflexively say A is also true given the condition, but that's actually wrong. A would only be true as well if only A is the *only sufficient condition* for B. A sufficient condition refers to a condition or set of conditions that, if satisfied, guarantees the occurrence or truth of a given outcome or result. To put in an example, raining is a sufficient condition for the outdoor playground to be wet. When the condition is met, the consequence is inevitable. However, to flip this the other way round; if the ground is wet, it doesn't necessarily have to be the result from rain. It could have been a result of the streets being cleaned. When we are trying to establish causality, it is important to consider the other possible factors that give rise to a certain phenomenon. We shouldn't make claims unless we can isolate the variables as best as we can by establishing sufficiency and exclusivity.

Other than sufficient conditions, in the realm of logic there is also a type of condition called necessary conditions. It is a condition or set of conditions that must be present or satisfied for a given outcome or result to occur. However, the mere presence of the factor doesn't guarantee the occurrence of the outcome as there are other factors or conditions that may contribute to or influence the occurrence of the outcome. Let's use an example to illustrate. Combustion requires oxygen, so the presence of an ongoing fire implies that there must be oxygen. Yet, the presence of oxygen doesn't mean there's a fire.

Here, we are flipping it around by saying that just because a factor exists doesn't mean a specific consequence will ensue. It is important for us not to jump to conclusions simply and the key to it is to thoroughly understand the concept of necessary conditions.

There are many more logic rules out there, and don't worry, I won't list all of them. Personally, I think knowing the distinction between necessary and sufficient conditions is already a great start as being able to tell the differences can already help ensure the validity of most of our arguments. By having the ability to make accurate and valid inferences and predictions, we shall be able to make better informed decisions and foster more constructive discussions.

Building Consensus: Overcoming Cognitive Dissonance

To embrace the discomfort when we encounter contradictory information and fight our tendencies to protect our beliefs are certainly not easy undertakings. But I believe that we owe it to ourselves and humanity to try our best. I firmly believe in rationalism, the power of humans to find answers using reason. *In fact, this is probably the only tool we can use because we can never make a truly informed decision but just a reasonable guess of what we should do next.* In the past, we used our power of reasoning to create abstract concepts such as morals, economy, religion, and politics to help us establish orders and stability.

Unfortunately, we are now in an era where the old ways of working and dogmas can't seem to keep up with the current world. Democracy and capitalism face unprecedented challenges. Moral dilemmas become increasingly complex, and geopolitical tensions remain inflamed, as evident in the Israel and Gaza Strip conflict. Moreover, the development of Artificial General Intelligence raises concerns about potential existential threats[44]. In light of these pressing issues, there is a great need to engage in open discussions and revisit our perspectives.

Therefore, it is crucial to train our minds to embrace differing opinions and possess the mental agility to change when necessary. Instead of being driven solely by emotional attachments to our own beliefs and perpetuating divisions between "us" and "them," progress can only be achieved through collective collaboration. Considering the extensive list of unresolved issues weighing on us, there is an urgent need to enhance the quality of our thought process. While it may be challenging in the beginning, it will get better with practice.

Turning the Tables - an Introduction to Part II

———

Congratulations! You've finished Part I of the book. Before we dive into Part II, let's summarize our learnings thus far.

In Chapter 1, we explored the Bayesian Brain Hypothesis, a theoretical framework in cognitive neuroscience that explains how we form perceptions and make decisions based on both prior beliefs and incoming sensory information. *This powerful design is the reason why we're the only species capable of learning, adapting, and anticipating.* However, this design also *predisposes us to cognitive biases* because our prior beliefs influence our perceptions, which may or may not be accurate.

Thankfully, the Bayesian Brain Hypothesis does allow for an update mechanism, so we always have the chance to rectify our beliefs should they detract from reality. However, there are other forces within us that hinder this update mechanism, as discussed in Chapters 2 to 4.

In Chapter 2, we discovered that *rectifying deeply ingrained beliefs is a biological challenge,* as it takes time to dismantle the reinforced neural pathways. Additionally, we explored how our *fear of uncertainty can be a powerful force deterring change.* This fear can generate a surge of nervous energy that, in some cases, drives individuals to form angry mobs simply due to their desire to cling to familiar aspects of life, even if the reality is far from ideal.

In Chapter 3, we explored the opposite aspect of fear, which is the anticipation of reward. As individuals, we possess an innate motivation to comprehend our environment as it is crucial for our survival. *Consequently, believing that we have the correct understanding of a situation and being proven right becomes a gratifying experience.* Nevertheless, it is this pursuit of the anticipated reward that often gives rise to confirmation bias. If we are not cautious and begin with incorrect assumptions, we can be led astray, far from the truth.

Throughout these chapters, I've encouraged readers to be less apprehensive about changes and to be more open-minded to contradictory information. However, this is easier said than done. In Chapter 4, we looked at how the sense of discomfort could lead us to rationalize any conflicting beliefs or behaviors, and *because we're so eager to reconcile the inconsistency, it's possible that we'd be blindsided from the invalidity of our arguments.* The force is so strong that it could create a reality that is completely detached from the truth, as if it were a parallel universe.

When we talk about cognitive biases, there's an assumption that we should always do our best to keep them in check because they're a bad thing. In the second half of the book, let me play the role of a devil's advocate. Instead of assuming that we should proactively keep our cognitive biases in check, let's also consider the arguments that suggest maybe we shouldn't try too hard.

In order to guard ourselves against the influence of biases, it is implied that we have to continuously assess the validity of our arguments and be willing to acknowledge when we are wrong. We will take a look at *whether our newfound caution and humility would take a toll on our confidence and assertiveness* in chapter 5 and chapter 6 respectively.

Setting aside potential negative impacts, it is important to consider the feasibility of countering our biases. Biases and emotions are intimately intertwined, as emotions are involuntary responses to our surroundings and experiences that give rise to biases by distorting our perceptions and tilting our judgments. The question then arises: *Can we truly negate the effects of emotions and maintain a level-headed perspective?* If achieving this seems like an insurmountable task, one may wonder if it is worthwhile to embark on the journey at all. This thought-provoking conundrum will be extensively explored and discussed in Chapter 7.

It may seem quite unorthodox to provide counterarguments against trying to reduce our cognitive biases, but I'm simply adhering to the principle that I advocated in chapter 3 - that we should consider multiple perspectives before we draw a conclusion.

So, without further ado, let us begin Part II of the book.

Chapter 5 - The Fine Line Between Confidence and Ignorance

———

Recently, the firm I worked at decided to open up a new position and I was responsible for the interviews. Many resumes flooded in, but only a handful stood out. One of which was particularly impressive. While the candidate did not graduate from a prestigious university, nor had he worked in international corporations such as the Big Four or the Big Techs, he was, at the age of 26 years old, a co-founder of an e-commerce platform for sex toys and supplements trading for 3 years. I knew I had to meet this candidate because I was really curious as to how he navigated the business world with very little experience, and why he was applying for jobs when he already had a pretty decent startup.

For days, I was looking forward to the interview. I was expecting an energetic, confident young man, who had a lot of interesting stories to share. However, as the interview commenced, I saw a rather timid person. His shoulders were slightly crouched, and he didn't look into the camera at all. For every question I asked, he would give a rather curt reply. All of these suggested to me that he was nervous and lacked confidence. Throughout the call, I took a more casual tone and asked questions that played to his strength, hoping that would help him loosen up. However, he remained rather hesitant and coy in his response. Seeing that he had no questions for us, I quickly wrapped up the interview after 20 minutes.

As two of my other teammates also sat in on the interview, so we had a debrief after the call. On one hand, we all agreed that he must be a fast learner or else he wouldn't be able to take up the burden of starting a business. On the other, he seemed to lack confidence and that, to us, was quite a red flag. In our day-to-day work, we need to project confidence so our stakeholders would trust our planning and executions. We need to project confidence so that our project sponsors would believe in our visions and approve budgets to support our roadmaps. While confidence alone is not going to get the job done, it is definitely an important, must-have quality. In the midst of uncertainty, a person who projects confidence is like a beacon of light in the darkness. It ensures others that the problems at hand would be solved eventually. *Confidence makes people hopeful and optimistic; it gives people comfort as they venture through the darkness and uncertainty that await.* It is a quality that leaders, or people who want to climb the corporate ladder must demonstrate.

Then there's a problem.

The Inverse Relationship Between Caution and Confidence

If there's a key message from my previous chapters, it is that *we shouldn't be giving our brains unequivocal trust*, and that we should be constantly checking and reflecting our thoughts and decisions to ensure that they're sound, valid, and unbiased. But if I can't even trust my perceptions or judgments, then how can I ever hope to project confidence?

I suspect this question may not be a popular one, because it is morally commendable to overcome our cognitive biases. *However, just because it's right doesn't mean we shouldn't be probing questions into the potential tradeoffs.* In psychology, there is a phenomenon called the Dunning Kruger Effect. It says that people who are blissfully unaware of their limitations and ignorance tend to overestimate their abilities and knowledge, and therefore exhibit higher confidence even when their actual competence is low[45]. On the other hand, individuals who are knowledgeable enough to know what they don't know tend to be more self-critical and thereby underestimate their own capabilities. This phenomenon, which is the polar opposite of the Dunning Kruger Effect, is called the Imposter Syndrome[46].

If we apply the phenomenon into the context of the book, there appears to be an inverse relationship between critical thinking or self-introspection and self-confidence. People who are not as aware of their biases and how the biases can lead them astray are expected to experience less self-doubt and therefore maintain a higher level of confidence even though they really should not. The case of Donald Trump is the perfect example. Even though he was extremely biased and ignorant to all sorts of issues, millions of people were attracted by his confidence and believed in him enough to vote for him as the President of the United States back in 2018. If projection of confidence is more valued than careful thought process and quality decisions, why should we bother to be so wary of our own thoughts at the expense of our confidence? When it comes to confidence, it seems like the Dunning Kruger effects and the Imposter syndromes are suggesting that the less careful you are on your thoughts, the more confident you can be.

Confidence: A Mystery

To address this dilemma, let's begin by defining what confidence is. *Confidence can be described as the belief and assurance in our own abilities, qualities, or judgments.* It is a state of mind that empowers us to approach tasks and challenges with a sense of certainty and optimism. While this concept may seem abstract, it holds great significance, leading to numerous articles, books, and courses attempting to transform this mystical quality into something more tangible.

Primarily, confidence is characterized by positivity. Consequently, various resources bombard their audience with positive messages such as "you can do it!" and "believe in yourself!" to foster encouragement and, more importantly, to foster self-belief. *Although these affirmations provide comfort, developing genuine beliefs takes time.* Nevertheless, societal norms tend to favor individuals who exude confidence. Therefore, in addition to the encouraging notes, these materials also offer a list of behaviors that project confidence. Suggestions may include standing tall, maintaining direct eye contact, using a strong and clear voice when speaking, and adopting a wide stance while sitting. By mimicking these behaviors, readers can outwardly display confidence without necessarily comprehending its true essence. The ultimate hope is that, gradually, individuals will no longer need to feign confidence because the display of confidence can attract opportunities and success. As achievements and accomplishments accumulate, true confidence can naturally emerge.

Fake it Till You Make It?

The game of poker comes to mind when considering the concept of make-belief. It is not necessary to possess the strongest hand to win; rather, it's crucial to create the *perception* that you hold the best hand, prompting other players to fold and allowing you to claim the pot. Consequently, many people associate poker with the art of bluffing. Novice players often adopt an aggressive betting strategy to convey strength, even when their hand is weak or non-existent. Unfortunately, they often neglect to consider the possibility of being called out on their bluff. Their sole focus is on projecting themselves as the player with the superior hand, without assessing the credibility of their façade.

However, if you're interested in learning poker, it's important to note that this strategy can *backfire dramatically*, especially when facing skilled opponents. Experienced players possess a reliable method of systematically narrowing down the range of possible cards and calculating the odds of winning. Based on their inferences from the opponent's bet size in different stages of the game, they can make informed decisions even without seeing their opponent's cards. If a bluffer chooses to persist in their deception by escalating their bets, they may lose all their chips in one round as a result.

Typically, when a bluffer experiences failure, it's common for them to lose their composure. They may attribute their lack of success to mere luck and decide to end their session for the night. Some might believe that their failure was a result of not being aggressive enough, leading them to buy in again and adopt an even more aggressive approach. Unfortunately, this often leads to further losses.

On the other hand, a skilled poker player approaches the game with composure. While they may not win every single round, their ability to carefully calculate odds and interpret betting patterns allows them to minimize uncertainty and maximize their gains. Instead of attributing losses solely to luck, they reflect on their gameplay and identify areas where they can improve their calculations. Despite experiencing fluctuations in their chip stack, they steadily build their bankroll over time.

Poker: The Game of Life

Out of all the gambling games, poker holds a special place as my favorite. Its dynamic nature often serves as an inspiration for navigating uncertainty with confidence in real life. Poker is designed in a way that forces us to make decisions with incomplete information. The essence of the game lies in finding ways to gather as much information as possible within those constraints and making the best decisions based on the information available.

Even if we hold a strong hand like a pair of Aces, we are not exempt from this need for information, as we have no control over the communal cards that will be revealed. Each time a new communal card is unveiled, we must carefully observe the betting patterns of our opponents, reassess our own hand strength, and, most importantly, be ready to adjust our strategies if necessary. While others may try to intimidate us, it is crucial to maintain composure and analyze whether their actions are a bluff, a trap, or a genuine threat. Furthermore, it is vital not to fold simply because we are uncertain or uncomfortable with the unknown. We must hold our heads high and remain confident in our ability to navigate through uncertainty and failure. Otherwise, we risk significant losses.

These parallel our experiences in life, where we are often confronted with decisions without complete information. The future is inherently uncertain, and the present is filled with distractions and noise. In such circumstances, our best course of action is to gather as much relevant information as possible to make informed decisions. *While we may not be able to succeed every time, we must not let uncertainty and failure deter us from experiencing life. To achieve all of these, we must control our minds, and learn to protect our perceptions and judgments from the influence of biases.* Instead of letting luck decide on our fate, our ability to think and decide for ourselves is what enables us to create the best outcomes for ourselves.

Confidence in the Face of Bias

With that note, it brings us back to our conundrum on the inverse relationship between careful thought process and level of confidence. *If confidence is defined as the trust in our own ability to complete tasks and solve problems, then countering biases and improving the quality of our thoughts and decisions are essential prerequisites, rather than deterrents, for building a strong foundation of self-confidence.* By making better decisions, we enhance our ability to effectively tackle challenges. Each time we successfully solve a problem, regardless of its size, we gain valuable experience. These experiences accumulate, providing our Bayesian Brain with a wealth of past records that enable it to predict our capability to handle new challenges. When our prior beliefs support our predictions, confidence naturally ensues.

What about the Dunning Kruger effect? It is true that individuals who lack awareness of their own ignorance often exhibit a higher level of confidence. It is also true that their confidence will experience a dip as they begin to realize the extent of what they don't know. However, the last part of the theory says that confidence level will increase again once we've accumulated sufficient learning and experiences.

Dunning–Kruger Effect

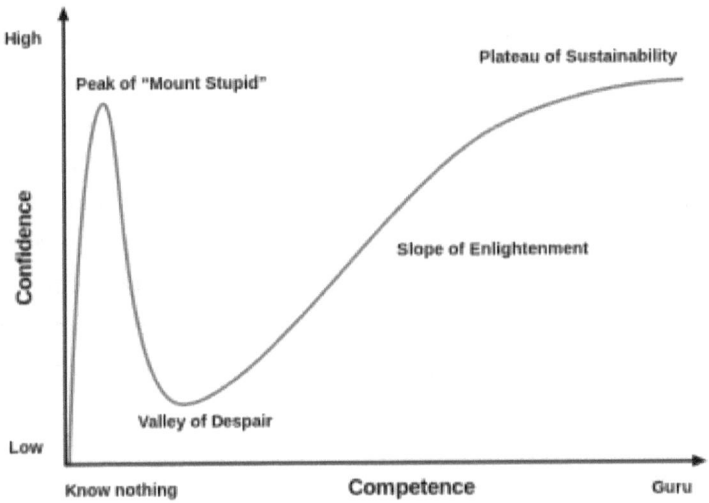

Illustration of Dunning-Kruger effect from Wikipedia[47]. As we acquire knowledge, we become increasingly aware of the vast amount of information and understanding that eludes us, leading us into the depths of the Valley of Despair. However, with perseverance, we gradually ascend the slope of enlightenment, eventually reaching the Plateau of Sustainability. On this plateau, we have attained a sufficient level of comprehension, allowing us to enhance our knowledge more effectively through continuous improvement.

Let us take a moment to reflect on our life journey. We all started with a blank state with absolutely no clue what was going on around us, let alone to solve any problems. But we are masters at pattern seeking, and we're able to log our experiences and learn from them. All of these contribute to our current capabilities and let us know ourselves better. *It is all of the knowledge and experience we've accumulated over time that allow us to become more assured and composed.* For example, when you first graduated, you may get very nervous about job interviews, but as you've hit your thirties and you've changed jobs a couple of times, you now see interviews as an opportunity to assess whether the position and company fit you, rather than just sitting there being assessed. Same goes with promotions. At first, you might not feel you were up to the job, and you worried that you would screw up spectacularly. But who's born a leader? With time and the willingness to learn and adapt, we would gain the necessary skills to navigate our new role with ease.

The same principle applies to the training of our thought processes. *Initially, it may be challenging and counterintuitive, but through consistent practice, we can achieve mastery.* Therefore, as we embark on the journey of understanding and overcoming cognitive biases, let's not view it as a threat to our confidence, but rather as an opportunity to deepen it. Let's embrace it as a chance to build a solid and reliable foundation for our beliefs and decisions—a foundation grounded in a clear-eyed understanding of how our brains function, with all their quirks and biases. *By doing so, we can cultivate true self-confidence, which is not about always being right but rather about being comfortable with being wrong and having the willingness and the tools to correct our course when needed.* There is no need for mimicry or bluffing anymore, for our confidence is firmly grounded in our genuine belief in our ability to assess, predict, resolve, and learn.

Building Confidence: A Balance of Understanding, Compassion, and Self-Improvement

Since you've gotten this far in the book, I am sure you, my dear readers, must have a will and strive to improve on the quality of your thinking. As you start to adopt a more critical perspective towards yourself and the world, please remember that just because you take a critical view on your thoughts doesn't mean you have to be the harsh inner critic that only focuses on failures and deficiency. Not only should confidence be rooted in understanding, rather than ignorance, it should only be rooted in acceptance and optimism that you can be even better. You don't have to worry about being an Imposter. The fact that you're taking the first step to recognize the influences of cognitive biases on your thinking is already better than a lot of people. Therefore, please continue in this journey with optimism. Believe in your brain's capability to learn and adapt. Rest assured that with time and dedication, you will gain mastery over your own mind, and attain a level of confidence that is rooted in both understanding and compassion, rather than ignorance and criticism.

Chapter 6 - The False Dichotomy of Collaboration and Strengths

In the preceding chapter, we dipped our toes into the potential downside of striving for rational, unbiased thinking: a temporary dip in confidence. However, we also acknowledged that in the long run, this approach improves the quality of our thought processes. It enables us to trust our judgments, laying the foundation for true, unshakeable confidence.

Now, let's explore another possible side effect of self-introspection and critical thinking. Here's a question that's always lurking in the back of my mind: As we strive to minimize bias, we naturally seek out as much information as possible, leading to frequent shifts in perspective. Over time, this might make it difficult for us to speak with conviction, knowing that today's truth could be tomorrow's falsehood. We might even hesitate to draw our own conclusions before we've heard from everyone else.

While these habits can foster critical thinking, active listening, and mental agility, they can also be seen as weaknesses during negotiations or conflicts. An aggressive opponent might take advantage of our humility and open-mindedness, dominating the conversation and imposing their will.

It's natural to want to defend ourselves during a negotiation or conflict. It's tempting to flex our muscles, literally or figuratively, to get the outcome we want. And it's especially easy to resort to brute force if our position gives us enough leverage. But I've found that by resisting the urge to reject change and opposing views, I've gained far more than I've given up.

Allow me to take you on my personal journey exploring this topic.

The Story of Project One

In 2018, I joined the digital team at a bank, led by an indomitable leader who I'll call Sarah. Known for her strong-willed and no-nonsense approach, Sarah led the team in adding over a hundred functionalities to the app within three years—a remarkable feat given the complexities of the banking industry.

All of this changed with the introduction of Project One. This initiative, mandated by the global team, aimed to standardize our mobile app across all markets. While this made sense from an organizational standpoint, Sarah saw it as a disruption to her roadmap and a threat to her team's autonomy. Unwilling to back down, she challenged the global team, criticizing their designs, and even threatened to withdraw unless they yielded to her demands. The ensuing debates and escalations fostered a hostile and apprehensive environment, with most discussions devolving into arguments and little productive progress.

But the global team was not the only challenge Sarah faced. Ronald, our tech lead, discovered compatibility issues between the new design and our existing systems. Resolving these issues would require three times more effort than initially anticipated. Faced with a choice to reduce scope or extend the timeline, Sarah rejected both options, citing her commitment to senior management.

As Sarah remained unwilling to make any concessions, Ronald and his team made a valiant attempt to catch up. However, they quickly came to the realization that it was simply impossible to complete the original scope within the given timeline. When they finally acknowledged their defeat, Sarah publicly chastised Ronald, placing the blame squarely on him and his team for the setbacks. This unfortunate turn of events escalated into a heated argument, with personal accusations being hurled back and forth. Ginny, the project manager, confronted Sarah, pointing out her unreasonable behavior and revealing that Sarah's unwavering attitude had become a significant source of stress for the entire team.

Ginny's comments, though painful, had a basis in truth. Sarah's aggressive leadership style had created friction and inefficiency within the team. Communication dwindled, morale plummeted, and productivity suffered. Technical completion of the project masked underlying issues; the lack of transparency and motivation led to quality problems that required substantial refactoring. The emotional toll was high, with even long-standing relationships, like Sarah and Ronald's, crumbling under the strain.

Positional Negotiation - the Default Strategy for Most People

Despite the emotional toll with putting on an aggressive facade, I believe that many individuals would have taken the same approach to Sarah's. It is natural to approach different matters from our own perspectives and ask ourselves, "What is in it for us?" As a result, whenever a conflict of interest arises, we often perceive the negotiation as a zero-sum game, where one party can only gain something at the expense of others. This perspective implies two things: making concessions will inevitably lead to losses, and there's no reason to listen because the counterparties are incentivized to coax, lie, and to manipulate. Consequently, positional negotiation becomes the default strategy. In this approach, we enter negotiations with a set of assumptions and a range of acceptable outcomes for ourselves[48]. We start with an extreme position, allowing room for concessions within our range. Since this strategy focuses on the position itself and assumes the other side as *the enemy*, we lack the incentive to understand the *underlying interests* of others. Our goal is simply to exploit and attack in order to safeguard our positions and maximize our gains. If our counterparts happen to be gentle and compliant, this strategy may work even better as we can potentially extract more value from them.

However, this approach backfired spectacularly in Project One. By assuming antagonism and showing no willingness to listen, it was only logical that the counterparts grew apprehensive. By lacking empathy for their challenges, it was only logical that the counterparts adopted similar strategies, caring only about their priorities and benefits. We became so vested in our own positions and interests that it didn't not even occur to us that we could have attempted to find some common ground between the two ranges. All of these because we are unaware that we have the wrong assumptions about others, about conflict resolutions. In the end, everyone lost. Despite successfully completing the initiative, there was no celebration. We were all exhausted and jaded, with bridges burned. It was difficult to envision future collaboration.

Perhaps that was the reason why both Sarah and Ronald chose to leave. Sarah transitioned to another department shortly after the project concluded, and Ronald resigned. I was deeply saddened by this outcome. What was the purpose of accomplishing something when the team was shattered? In our highly complex world, collaboration becomes essential as we borrow each other's strengths on multiple occasions. *It is the people that we work with that gives us the power to transcend our own limitations and solve a problem that we cannot tackle alone.*

An Experiment on Collaboration

A year later, I decided to leave the bank's mobile team, which felt unfamiliar without Sarah and Ronald, and join a tech startup. However, within the first few weeks at my new company, I noticed a familiar dynamic between the product and technical teams. The product side was aggressively pressing the technical team to shorten the timeline without making any concessions on the scope, reminiscent of the conflict in Project

One. On the other hand, the technical team was fiercely pushing back.

This conflict was foreseeable, given the nature of the roles. Product managers strive to accomplish more within shorter timeframes and at lower costs, while developers aim to build technically robust systems that cater to even the most exceptional scenarios. To complicate matters, our technical development was outsourced to a vendor who charges based on man-days, akin to how lawyers charge by the hour. Therefore, the product and business teams often assumed that the vendor was inflating the timeline to increase the contract value.

Seeing this situation as an opportunity to test a collaborative approach despite opposing interests, I volunteered to lead communication with the technical team. I started by sharing my vision for the application and invited the technical team to co-create the implementation details. I made a point to recap their suggestions to demonstrate understanding, which encouraged them to explain their rationale too. As we developed mutual understanding of our standpoints, we were able to prioritize a scope that fit the timeline and aligned with my vision.

While this collaborative approach required more time than simply issuing orders, it proved invaluable in formulating a plan that both parties felt comfortable with. Not only did I gain valuable technological knowledge, but I was also able to spend less time contemplating solutions because the technical team was able to provide sensible recommendations when we encountered issues. The alliance that emerged from this collaboration was unexpected; the technical lead became my most trusted advisor, and his team even completed tasks ahead of schedule. Consequently, we expanded the scope from one app to three. The experiment was undeniably a resounding success, proving that collaboration can triumph over conflict.

Interest-Based Negotiation: Everything is on the Table

This experience has been pivotal for me, as it made me realize that the setup of our roles and positions, which often creates conflicts of interest that we cannot change, does not stop us from collaborating with one another. *Beneath the surface of the dichotomy, there are mutual underlying interests we can explore and fulfill.* This is the essence of the interest-based negotiation approach. Instead of fixating on predefined positions and preconceived notions, interest-based negotiation requires active listening and intellectual empathy among participants[49]. *This allows us to listen to the other parties and identify the underlying interests and needs of all parties involved, so that we can collectively work towards a solution that satisfies everyone's needs.* Unlike positional negotiation, which focuses internally on our own demands, this approach encourages us to reassess our assumptions about what the other side wants and adapt our perspectives based on new information received during the conversation. This shift in approach from a 'win-lose' to a 'win-win' mindset not only preserves relationships but often leads to *more innovative and sustainable outcomes.*

But would there be a case where the underlying interests simply cannot be satisfied?

While I cannot guarantee that external rewards such as money, power, and fame will always align, there is one underlying interest that is universally shared and deeply ingrained in our brains: *the desire to be heard and respected.* Throughout the course of evolution, our brains have developed a strong drive for human connection. Our physical vulnerability necessitates working together to enhance our chances of survival. After all, breaking a single stick is easy, but breaking a bundle of sticks becomes challenging. *Thus, we are inherently wired as social beings.* To incentivize and facilitate our bonding with others, we possess a fundamental need to be heard and understood. We are naturally inclined to build rapport and form alliances. When we feel heard and respected, our brains release a cascade of happy hormones[50], including oxytocin, serotonin, endorphins, GABA, and dopamine, which provide a sense of relaxation and well-being. This internal reward system can shift our priorities, sometimes outweighing typical external rewards.

Let's delve into an example within the realm of Human Resources to illustrate these dynamics. Employees often desire a higher salary, while management is driven by the need to protect profits, creating a conflicting situation where employees want something (money) that management is often reluctant to provide. These common dynamic leads many to believe that low pay is the primary reason for employee resignations. However, research has revealed that low pay is just one of the main factors driving employees away; feeling disrespected in the workplace is equally influential[51]. This understanding has sparked a growing trend in the corporate world, where organizations prioritize mental well-being and cultivate positive working environments. Instead of solely focusing on salary negotiations, Human Resources departments now consider other underlying interests that can enhance the attractiveness of their company. This shift highlights the significance of feeling respected and heard, and it exemplifies the application of interest-based negotiation to address conflicts of interest.

Defense Against the Dark Arts

Before we fully embrace the collaborative approach as a foolproof solution to disagreements and conflicts, it's important to recognize its limitations. The success of interest-based negotiation relies heavily on whether your counterpart is also willing to adopt this approach. Operating in good faith does not guarantee reciprocation, as many still perceive negotiation as a cutthroat process. A collaborative stance can be mistaken as a sign of weakness, potentially inviting unscrupulous tactics. Therefore, it is essential to learn how to defend against these 'dark arts.' Some common tactics include:

- Overgeneralization[52] - Drawing conclusions or beliefs based on limited or insufficient evidence and applying them to a broader range of situations or individuals. For example, having a negative experience with one team member and generalizing that the entire team is incompetent.

● Oversimplification[53] - Failing to consider the complexity of problems and fixating on a single aspect. Seeing negotiation as a zero-sum game is an example of oversimplification. This type of thinking focuses on one factor, such as financial implications, while ignoring other factors like quality of services, reputation, or brand value.

● False Dichotomy[54] - Presenting a complex issue as having only two mutually exclusive options or outcomes, disregarding alternative choices or shades of gray. For instance, insisting that a person either accept all conditions during a negotiation or the deal is off, without considering potential middle ground.

● Semantic Distortion - A range of tactics that distort or misinterpret the meaning of words or concepts to manipulate others' perceptions. One common tactic is the straw man fallacy[55], misrepresenting or distorting an argument to make it easier to attack or refute. For example, if you try to give others a chance to speak during a conversation dominated by someone, they may accuse you of being authoritarian and trying to suppress freedom of speech.

These tactics not only aim to undermine your positions and arguments but can also provoke frustration and cause you to lose your composure. Instead of falling for these tactics, call them out. *Developing strong listening and critical thinking skills is essential to identifying and exposing these invalid arguments.* If you can pinpoint exactly where their arguments falter, you can clarify your meaning and restate your arguments to set the record straight.

If your counterpart persists in their attack, suggest refocusing the conversation on the agreed-upon agenda. This can help steer the discussion back on track. However, if they escalate with more aggressive behaviors like constant interruptions, intimidation, personal attacks, or insults, *communicate your expectations for a respectful and constructive conversation firmly.* If necessary, be prepared to walk away from the discussion until they can conduct themselves appropriately. Remember, there is a difference between being collaborative and being a doormat. Knowing when to walk away is vital to avoid exploitation.

Humanity Unified: Embracing Collaboration for Collective Progress

After reading about my experiences and tips, I hope that I have successfully debunked two misconceptions. *Firstly, it is important to understand that being willing to listen and empathize with others during arguments or negotiations is <u>not</u> a sign of weakness.* In fact, it is a necessary prerequisite for engaging in a more effective form of negotiation known as interest-based negotiation. This approach focuses on finding solutions that address the underlying interests of all participants, leading to a sustainable and mutually beneficial agreement. Instead of being locked into our initial belief of what the other side wants, we shall be ready to revise our initial assumptions as we listen and intellectually empathize. By doing that, we inherently fulfilled one underlying interest that makes collaboration possible, and that is the hardwired need of humans for being listened to and respected.

Secondly, adopting an approach that seeks to address underlying interests does not mean disregarding our own needs, nor does it require sacrificing ourselves to please others. *As we voice our opinions and demands, we can do so in a direct and confident manner while simultaneously showing respect for others.* It is imperative that others understand and respect the rules of engagement, aiming for collaboration. If anyone attempts to dominate or intimidate, it is crucial to call out such behavior and establish clear boundaries. This is the one principle that should always be upheld, and this is the foundation for assertiveness.

Although the examples in the chapter mainly focus on the work aspect, it is important to understand that these new perspectives can also be applied to our personal interactions. *Negotiation applies to more than just contracts; it encompasses any situation where two or more parties are trying to work together despite differing opinions.* Whether it's discussing division of household chores or deciding on a location for a party with friends, *negotiation is inherent in seeking alignment.* If we persist in dominating even in personal engagements, aggression will eventually lead to resentment and alienation, and there's only so many times where your aggression can prevail before you alienate yourself from everyone.

I recognize that interest-based negotiation may not be the most intuitive approach, but I assure you that implementing it can significantly improve your quality of life. By embracing a mindset of listening and accommodation, we create a more inclusive and collaborative environment. Consensus becomes easier to reach, a stronger sense of belonging is fostered, and concerns about negative outcomes diminish as our goals become aligned and integrated with others.

In reflecting on the journey from the adversarial battlegrounds of Project One to the collaborative triumphs in my startup experience, it becomes clear that the ability to collaborate effectively is not separate from, but rather *an extension of, rational, unbiased thinking*. By applying the principles of critical introspection and thoughtful analysis to our interactions with others, we unlock the potential for collective progress. This is not merely a negotiation strategy but a fundamental approach to addressing the complex, interconnected challenges we face, whether in our professional lives or the global issues that await us.

Chapter 7 - Taming the Emotional Beast: Regulating Emotions to Mitigate Biases

We have finally arrived at the final chapter. Throughout this book, we've embarked on a journey to understand cognitive biases from a neuroscience perspective. Our goal was not only to demystify the imperfections of humanity but also to minimize them. From the very start of our journey, we understood that we are wired to be biased. Changing this goes against our instinct. Not that it's impossible, but it does require cognitive effort, and the journey to mastery isn't easy. Naturally, one might question whether it's worth the effort. In the previous two chapters, we discussed the potential impacts of bias on our self-confidence and assertiveness during negotiation and conflicts. After careful reflection, it's safe to conclude that while the adverse impacts exist, they're often short-term. In contrast, the long-term benefits far outweigh the costs: we will be able to embrace uncertainty because true confidence lies in our ability to find a path when no one else can, and we will be able to lay down our defenses because we've learned that collaboration is a far more effective and sustainable way of resolving conflicts.

Now that we have established the reasons to keep our cognitive biases in check, we shall move on to the final and most fundamental question: *is it even possible to overcome our biases?* Let's not forget that our biases are not just a limitation of our knowledge, but also propelled by our emotions. Our fear can make us relentlessly reject a change in belief in spite of solid evidence. Our sense of relief when we feel validated can make us seek out things that only support our version of the story. Our discomfort when challenged by contradictions can even lead us to create a whole parallel universe completely detached from reality. *If anything, emotions are the real culprits of cognitive biases.* However mild they appear to be, they hold the ability to warp our perceptions and tilt our judgments completely undetected. They set the tone of our reality and define our preferences and approaches. Worst of all, they are automatically triggered, and there's no stopping them because we'd only be aware of their existence *after* the neurotransmitters and the hormones have already been released[56]. We can only infer our emotional state based on the physiological and psychological changes that are results of the biochemical reactions. When that's the case, *can we genuinely fight against the influence of our emotions?*

The Unruly Nature of Emotions

I've spent my life trying to address that particular question. I have always been a cynical, angry person, even from a young age. All my life, I was plagued by a litany of rage episodes. When I was in primary school, I threw a chair at one of my classmates because he refused to obey my order as the prefect. When I was in secondary school, I told my Chinese History teacher to get lost in front of the whole class because I disagreed with her grading scheme. I even smacked someone's head with a badminton racket really hard because she accidentally hit me with a ball but didn't apologize. The episodes of rage might have quieted down a little bit during college because I genuinely enjoyed the period, but they worsened again after I graduated and moved back to Hong Kong. I remember tearing a proposal apart in front of my boss just because I really wanted to complete the deal, but he refused to support me.

Ancient philosopher Plato describes emotions using the Chariot Allegory[57], and it goes as follows: imagine we are on a chariot with two horses, trying to ascend to the "realm of eternal truths and form". Unfortunately, the two horses we have don't coordinate well with one another. One is white and noble, representing rationality, self-control, and virtues. Another is dark and rugged, representing the emotions, desires, and appetites. While the white horse understands where we want to go and is happy to cooperate to get us to the destination, the unruly dark horse would just roam wherever it wants to, leading us astray.

For me, it was clear that I wasn't able to control the chariot because my rugged, dark horse was just too wild and powerful. Because of my anger management issues, I've hurt so many people and managed to alienate myself from friends, partners, and mentors. I had very few friends growing up and had no one to turn to when I needed help. It was an incredibly lonely and stressful life. I knew I had to find a way to rein in this unruly dark horse of mine, or I was sure to fail in life.

But I did not know how.

In Search for a Way

When I shared this problem with the handful of friends that I had, some suggested that I should lower my expectations so that I won't get irritated when things don't go the way I planned. Others went a step further, suggesting that I should stop caring altogether, as we never react to things we don't care about. While there's certainly truth in both statements, I found it challenging to simply tone down my expectations or passion. *That would suggest a rather dim life—forgoing anger, but also excitement and motivation.* After all, anger is fueled by the desire to overcome challenges that block me from achieving my goals. If there's nothing that I care about or have expectations for, it's true that I probably won't get angry anymore. But there would also be nothing to strive for, nothing to look forward to. It's true that I won't get hurt or frustrated, but *what kind of life would I be living if there's no trust or hope?*

Since I wasn't able to find an answer for years, I gradually accepted the fact that I was always going to be an angry person. I blamed it on my genes; there must be something that makes me more susceptible to anger. Studies have shown that certain genes, such as the low functioning of monoamine oxidase A, have been associated with increased aggression[58]; perhaps I have the same problem. But above all, I blamed it on my childhood, because my mother was a temperamental, harsh, and controlling person who constantly abused me both verbally and physically even when I was a straight A student. For a very long time, anger was the only emotion I knew of. It became my default approach in order to express myself, and to terrorize people into giving me what I wanted.

Nonetheless, the loss of hope didn't stop me from reading materials about emotions. I supposed, deep down, I never gave up on finding an answer. And one day, it dawned on me that I had been looking at emotions wrongly all along. Despite their automatic nature, and their ability to bend reality, there were still ways for me to live with them without letting them control or define me.

The True Nature of Emotion

As I've mentioned, it's true that emotions are automatic, and we only realize *after* the fact that the biochemical reactions are all in motion. Let's go through some examples. We infer that we are angry when we notice our heart beats faster than usual and that we have the desire to overpower whatever blocks us. We only recognize these signs because our amygdala has triggered a cascade of responses and ultimately resulted in cortisol entering into our bloodstream, making our heartbeat faster[59]. Fear is similar; we infer that we are frightened by the fact that our heart is racing based on the fight or flight mechanism. The only difference is that instead of wanting to overpower the blockades, there is a desire for us to exit the situation. Happiness, on the other hand, is a result of the doings of the happy hormones which trigger a sense of joy and physical behaviors such as smiling. All of these examples suggest that emotions are essentially labels we created to describe the set of physiological and psychological states we are in, and these states are results of the interactions of our neurotransmitters and hormones with the rest of our bodies.

Having said that, it's easy to fixate on the automatic nature of emotions and conclude that there's no way to prevent them from happening. Whenever we hit the right trigger, be it spiders, demanding bosses, a cute basket of puppies, the corresponding emotions arise and there's no stopping them. But there's one thing we ought to remember about emotions - they are *transient*. Under normal circumstances, our body will not keep releasing the neurotransmitters or hormones - they simply can't and won't. A primary principle that underlies our bodily function is homeostasis, which is a self-regulating mechanism that ensures fluctuation in our body is kept at a narrow range, and that it will always return to baseline[60]. This mechanism has a wide range of applications, including blood sugar, oxygen, proteins, temperature, etc., and of course, it also applies to hormones and neurotransmitters through reuptake and degradation mechanisms, which we don't have to go into detail about. The important thing is the implication of such a mechanism - it means that with time, our emotions will subside, and we will return to baseline[61].

All We Need is Time

With that said, time is the great equalizer, a natural remedy when it comes to emotional regulation. The strategy becomes much clearer. *All we need to do is to bid ourselves more time and also shorten the time needed for the emotions to wane.* So, exactly how much time do we need? It depends. Nonetheless, let's take a look at a better researched response - fight or flight response - as a reference. Research suggests that it generally takes around 20 to 60 minutes for the body to return to its normal state after the stress response is activated[62]. So next time when you're angry or stressed, consider taking a walk or going for a coffee break. Before you make any decisions or contemplate further, give yourself time to wait for the biochemical cascades to subside.

However, the above research could only serve as a reference point. We need to keep in mind that *different intensities of emotion would have different cooling off periods*, and they do not necessarily have to follow the aforementioned range. For example, if a stranger accidentally bumped you in the metro, you probably would be irritated due to the violation of personal space (I know I would be). Nonetheless, as this is only a mild transgression, the anger usually dissipates quickly if they apologize or move away. The fluctuation is so mild that it doesn't even have to take 20 minutes to dissipate the stress hormones and stop the cascade.

Now, let's take another scenario to another extreme. Imagine you are angry because you had a heated discussion with your parents, relatives, or partners, and they simply wouldn't listen to you and kept twisting your words. This level of anger may persist for a duration arguably much longer than 60 minutes. The last time I had a fight with my parents in the midst of the 2019 Anti-Extradition Protest over the topic of freedom to protest and police brutality, I was so upset at their remarks that I searched for an apartment to lease right away and moved out in two weeks. That wasn't the end of my rage, though; I held a grudge for an entire year in which I refused to talk to them or see them.

Stickiness of Emotion

Well, if it takes a year to appease my anger, can we still say that emotions are transient? Yes, and here's why. *When we experience a prolonged episode of emotions, it's not because the biochemical reactions persist.* It's not like the amygdala stays activated and is constantly triggering the production of stress hormones. It's not like the happy hormones keep activating neurons indefinitely. *The stickiness of the emotion comes from the fact that we keep re-triggering it[63].* Let's go back to the example of the rude stranger from the metro who didn't apologize after he accidentally bumped into you. Instead of him leaving the train, in this scenario, he stays and stands next to you. You may be able to let it go the first time, but just as your anger has subsided, he bumps into you again, for whatever reason. Not only is the anger response once again triggered, but the intensity has also increased. As you're brooding on the side, trying to tell yourself that this is completely normal in a busy metropolitan such as Hong Kong, this inconsiderate stranger bumped into you the third time. You've had enough and you confront him. Now this escalated into an argument with both sides exchanging heated words. Fortunately, that person had to get off at the next stop, so the fight was cut short. Later that day, when you shared this encounter with your friends, you realized you were angry again. You could feel your heart beating faster, your breathing hastening, and your face flushing.

Although no one is bumping into you anymore, and this rude stranger isn't standing right next to you, *simply reliving the moment that resulted in your frustration is enough to activate the anger response again.*

This is the intriguing thing about our brain. When we think about or recall past events, we're essentially triggering the neural pathways that recorded those events and the associated emotional response[64]. To the brain, as long as the neural pathways are activated, even if it's just a thought, a recollection, or an interpretation, it wouldn't matter. The pathway would then trigger the same emotional responses just because this is how the brain is built. *The differentiation between internal experiences and external reality can be blurry.*

If even a thought is enough to reset the clock, we can have all the time in the world and we still won't be able to escape from the recurring emotional episodes. That means one thing: we can't just simply wait for the emotion to subside. We need to devise strategies to *shorten the cool-down period and stop the retriggering so we can break free from the vicious cycle.*

Prefrontal Cortex: The Hallmark of Human Cognition

Before we go any further, let me first introduce the most important part of the brain - the prefrontal cortex. It is our executive control center[65] that allows us to perform goal-directed behavior, including analyzing, planning, and decision-making, and because of that, this is the component that makes us rational. *More importantly, by enabling us to deliberate, we are free to go beyond the default responses.* This, I think, is what separates humans from animals.

Let's take an example. When a cat feels frightened but trapped in a situation, you can reasonably anticipate its responses as it's limited. It'd probably bare its teeth, snarl, and swat with its paws. But humans are different, *humans have a very wide range of responses depending on the context and also the person himself.* For instance, let's say you're scared because the boss is yelling at people during a meeting and you're afraid you'd be next. While you may not have control over your bodily reactions, i.e., your pupils would still dilate, and your heart would still beat faster, you won't be snarling like a cat does. You certainly won't just leave in the middle of the meeting. *That's because our prefrontal cortex is working in the background to assess the situation and anticipate the consequences of our potential responses.* It knows that this meeting is not a life-threatening situation, so there's no reason to just leave. It also knows that social norms dictate that we can't just excuse ourselves from a meeting just because we can't stand the yelling. While the fight or flight responses would dictate a scared cat to react by showing aggression, the prefrontal cortex in us can put a brake on this circuit and come up with the third option, which is to mentally prepare what we have to say next, so we won't be the next target.

That is why the prefrontal cortex is the hallmark of human cognition. *Just because the underlying biochemical reactions are determined, it doesn't mean our responses are necessarily limited and determined.* While the prefrontal cortex cannot change our bodily reactions as the emotion arises, *it has the ability to press pause on whatever our emotions propel us to do* and take a more rational and analytical approach towards our issues. Instead of purely reacting to triggers in a way dictated by our biology, we have a choice on how we think it's best to resolve the problems. If we are able to defuse the situation and overcome the challenges, then the trigger is no more. We can then break free from the supposedly never-ending cycles.

Not Fast Enough

I suppose we've always known the power of the prefrontal cortex in emotional regulation. While Plato might not have stated the word "prefrontal cortex", it's obvious that the white horse in his Chariot analogy describes exactly what our executive control center does - it analyzes, it deliberates, and most importantly, it inhibits our emotion from running wild and leading us astray. If this is not a secret, why are most of us still encumbered by our unruly emotions?

Most people may attribute this to personality differences. Some people are born with good EQ (Emotional intelligence) while some are really bad at controlling their emotions. While I couldn't deny that genetics does play a role[66], the fundamental reason for how our emotions can take over and control us is actually the architecture of our brain.

Not only is our prefrontal cortex the most powerful component in the brain, but it is also part of the latest addition, neocortex, from evolution. This is probably why the prefrontal cortex is located *furthest away from our brainstem*[67], the most ancient part of the brain that relays commands from the brain to the rest of the body. Due to the distance, it will take time before a signal originates from the prefrontal cortex to reach the brainstem. Let's say we want to reach for a cup, your prefrontal cortex would have to first send a signal to the motor cortex, which then translates and passes on to the brainstem[68]. This transmission of signals is not a straightforward path.

On the other hand, the part of the brain that's responsible for our emotional response - the amygdala, has a much faster way to broadcast its signals to the rest of the body. Not only is it located closer to the brainstem, but it also has a direct connection with multiple components in the brainstem called the amygdalofugal pathway[69]. Once it generates an emotional response, it can directly communicate to the rest of the body for reactions.

The difference in the proximity to the brainstem and the presence of a direct connection means that it is possible for us to act on our emotional response *before* the prefrontal cortex has the time to deliberate and respond differently. Let's take an example. If you think there's a spider in your living room, your amygdala will quickly trigger a fear response and you'd immediately scream and fall back, without considering where you are and who you are with. The actions of screaming and falling back do not involve any conscious deliberation; this is just you purely reacting based on emotion. It's only after about another minute that you'd start thinking about possible resolutions. All of these aren't really your fault; *it just takes time to reach the prefrontal cortex, and it'd take more time for the prefrontal cortex to respond.*

To make things worse, cortisol - the stress hormones released during the fight or flight response can inhibit prefrontal cortex activity, making it difficult to process the situation, let alone to deliberate[70]. This effect is particularly obvious when the threat is intense. I remembered that one time when I was practicing combat with a senior in my Wing Chun lessons, I got hit on the face really hard. Immediately I could feel the burning sensation on my cheek. My heart raced even faster, and my eyes started to tear up. I kept trying to wrestle for control by telling myself to focus on the practice and find ways not to be hit again. As I was mustering all my strength trying to suppress my anger, he hit my face again. Now I could feel my lips trembling. I started throwing out more powerful punches at a faster rate. In retrospect, I guess I really wanted to beat the crap out of him, but it was really difficult because he was much taller and broader than me. Then, he hit me for the third time. This time I just lost it. I pushed him away and shouted "enough", and I walked to the bathroom to wash my face, hoping to calm myself down, but it was really difficult because my level of stress hormones must have been through the roof at the moment. I kept telling myself that he didn't mean it and I should let it go, but it was very hard when my cheek kept burning and my tears kept dropping. That was the time when I felt the might of our emotions. No matter how hard I tried to stay rational, the prefrontal cortex just felt out of reach.

The Power of "What Now?"

After some time, another classmate knocked on the door and asked if I was doing okay. I looked at the mirror and I thought to myself, "Ok, what now?" Somehow, this interruption extricated me from the impasse I had put myself in. The moment I asked myself what I should do next, my tears stopped, and my heart rate returned to normal. I could think straight again. I opened the bathroom door and said I was fine. When that guy apologized, I simply said, "Apology accepted" and patted him on the shoulder. I knew he wasn't being intentionally harmful, and we all needed to move on from this incident. Though my cheek was still burning, and it stayed that way for a whopping two hours, my anger had long subsided.

When I thought about this incident again, I realized that the key to emotional regulation is not to command ourselves to be rational. This is not a command that the prefrontal cortex recognizes. The only way to engage our prefrontal cortex is to focus on problem-solving. *By asking yourself "What now?", you are shifting your attention from the emotion itself to problem-solving and decision-making.* It takes your focus away from what has happened to what you need to do now. *You're encouraging yourself to formulate a response, and that's the cue for the prefrontal cortex to take the center stage.* As it enters to take charge, it will naturally send signals to inhibit our emotional responses, giving us the time and mental space needed to deliberate and do what we do best - analyze, plan, and deliberate.

At first, this might still feel a bit difficult and counterintuitive, but please don't be discouraged and definitely don't give up. *Our brain is just like any muscles in our body. The more you use it, the stronger it gets*[71]. By continuing our practices on emotional regulations, naturally more neural pathways will be built and connections with the prefrontal cortex will also strengthen. As mentioned in chapter 2, the more frequently utilized pathways will grow more dendrites and receptors to enhance signal transmission efficiency. Some may even have a myelin sheath as an insulation coating to minimize signal loss, making it even more efficient. *Our job is to persist in our practice so that we make the entry of the prefrontal cortex during stressful times as efficient as possible.* In Plato's words, this is how we tame the unruly horse and ensure our ascend to enlightenment.

A Final Note

As we reach the end of our journey, let's take a moment to reflect on the insights and lessons we've gathered along the way. We've delved into the intricacies of cognitive biases, explored their roots in neuroscience, and seen how they can subtly shape our thoughts, decisions, and interactions. We've taken a hard look at our own minds and confronted the uncomfortable truth that our thinking is not as rational and unbiased as we might like to believe.

Throughout this book, we've explored a range of strategies for mitigating the effects of cognitive biases—from cultivating self-introspection and critical thinking to regulating our emotions and adopting an interest-based approach to negotiation. We've seen that while our cognitive biases are a part of our human nature, we don't necessarily have to be constrained by them. With understanding, self-awareness, and practice, we can learn to navigate our biases and make better, more informed decisions.

We've also acknowledged the role of emotions in shaping our perceptions and judgments. We've learned that managing our cognitive biases isn't just about rational thinking—it also requires us to understand and regulate our emotional responses. By practicing emotional regulation and focusing on problem-solving, we can engage our prefrontal cortex, and the magic follows: we can then inhibit our emotional signals, mitigate the effects of our cognitive biases, and steer our thought processes in a more constructive and rational direction.

As we close this book, let's remember that understanding our cognitive biases is a lifelong journey. There's always more to learn, more biases to uncover, and more strategies to develop. But hopefully, this book has armed you with the knowledge and tools you need to start navigating your cognitive biases more effectively.

Thank you for embarking on this journey with me. As you move forward, I encourage you to keep questioning, keep learning, and keep striving for better understanding. The path to overcoming cognitive biases is not easy, but it is undoubtedly a worthy pursuit. Let's unchain ourselves and break free from the constraints of our biological designs.

Epilogue

First of all, I'd like to extend my heartfelt appreciation to you, the readers, for your support and engagement. I hope you found the journey through this book as enlightening as I did. Now that we've finished the lessons, let me share the making of the book.

The start of the journey went back to the 2019 Anti-Extradition Law protest in Hong Kong. I was deeply distressed by the stark divide that forever split us into two camps: pro government or pro protestors. The Internet brimmed with propaganda, accusations, and rancorous discussion from both sides. We were all reduced to a simply political view. Relations ended, friends became strangers, and families were torn apart. As I mentioned in earlier chapters, I, too, experienced a rift with my family due to this divide. The fact that we seemed to exist in different realities was deeply painful and frustrating. It felt as though we were physically in the same city and spoke the same language, yet we couldn't see or feel the same things. This disconnect propelled me to delve into the root of our disagreements and conflicts.

I immediately delved into psychology papers and philosophical books. While they offered some understanding of humanity and our weaknesses, something still felt missing. For instance, understanding the Dunning Kruger Effect explained why confidence could exist without any basis of competence or knowledge, but it didn't address why such a dynamic exists in the first place. Reading about various branches of philosophy provided a framework for approaching moral issues, but these theories were highly influenced by the context of history. What was valid as an argument back then might not necessarily be valid today. Consequently, I turned to neuroscience, adopting a first-principles approach. If perspectives and judgments originate from our brains, then this was where I needed to investigate.

Immersing myself with online neuroscience lectures and research, I came across Bayesian Brain Theory. With the help of this theory, I've started developing an understanding of our inherent constraints and why we do what we do. We are bound by what we know and have experienced, and we have a tendency to reconcile the differences between our predictions, or expectations, and reality. While neural plasticity offers us a means to change our belief, we don't necessarily do that because our emotion exerts an undue influence.

This led to a sobering conclusion: disagreement and conflicts are inevitable. This explains why our history is filled with blood and violence. We are propelled by our biology, a force which we have no control over, to perpetuate the cycle of hurting and fighting one another. This is truly a bitter pill to swallow.

Having trouble accepting this grim reality, I ventured into the realm of free will and determinism, which is highly contentious and no less tormenting. Some argue that there is no such thing as free will, while some assert that we must have control over our actions. Despite the compelling theories that indicate determinism, I yearned to prove the possibility of free will. However, Benjamin Libet's experiment[72], which suggests that decisions are made in the brain before we are consciously aware of them, shattered my last bit of hope. This experiment was a rather conclusive proof for me to accept that there's no free will.

However, an interview with Robert Sapolsky[73] offered a glimmer of hope. While he was one of the biggest advocates of determinism, he proposed that we could still be changed by our circumstances. *By seeing what others have achieved, we're changing the perceptions of our own possibility.* If others can do it, maybe I can do it too.

This brought me back to the Bayesian Brain Theory. While it is true that our neural firings are determined by our genes, hormones, history, and current circumstances, and that our consciousness is merely a playback of what has already transpired in our brain, our perception and decision-making are fundamentally about data and probability. We can trust our ability to learn, be it from our own experiences or from others. What once seemed impossible becomes possible because we've seen evidence of it elsewhere. *Just because we can't initiate change volitionally, it doesn't mean we can't change at all.* It all starts with beliefs. Once we believe that we can change, we set ourselves on a path of exploration that expands our own limits and possibilities. We start seeking environments conducive to change and altering our environments to reinforce the changes we make. *Despite the mechanistic framework that binds our body and mind, we are not entirely powerless.*

And so, I wrote this book. I wanted to share my journey - from a cynic who saw the worst in people to a hopeful individual who believes in progress and possibilities. I wanted to share the tools and strategies that enabled this transformation, in the hope that you too might find the *faith, will, and means* to embark on your own transformative journey.

Remember, we are the authors of our own stories, and we can choose the narratives that we wish to leave behind. Let's not be shackled by our biology but leverage it to overcome our biases to learn, and most importantly, to grow.

Thank you again for joining me on this journey.

References

Centers for Disease Control and Prevention, "Achievements in Public Health, 1990-1999: Healthier Mothers and Babies", https://www.cdc.gov/mmwr/preview/mmwrhtml/mm4838a2.htm

[2] Linda Hall Library, "Scientist of the day Ignaz Semmelweis", https://www.lindahall.org/about/news/scientist-of-the-day/ignaz-semmelweis/

[3] Karamanou M, Panayiotakopoulos G, Tsoucalas G, Kousoulis AA, Androutsos G, "From miasmas to germs: a historical approach to theories of infectious disease transmission". Infez Med. 2012 Mar;20(1):58-62. PMID: 22475662.

[4] Harry Bakery, "Climate "point of no return" may be much closer than we thought", https://www.space.com/climate-tipping-points-closer-than-realized

[5] Noback CR, Strominger NL, Demarest RJ, Ruggiero DA (2005). "The Human Nervous System: Structure and Function (Sixth ed.)". Totowa, NJ: Human Press. ISBN 1-59259-730-0.

[6] Kaas JH. "The Skinny on Brains: Size Matters. Cerebrum". 2018 May 1;2018:cer-06-18. PMID: 30746024; PMCID: PMC6353109.

[7] Xu Y. Limitations of object-based feature encoding in visual short-term memory. J Exp Psychol Hum Percept Perform. 2002 Apr;28(2):458-68. doi: 10.1037//0096-1523.28.2.458. PMID: 11999866.

[8] Harris Nathel, "Introduction to Bayesian Theorem", https://medium.com/@hmnathel/intro-to-bayes-theorem-8378648337fa (Accessed on May 7, 2023)

[9] Bottemanne H, Longuet Y, Gauld C. L'esprit predictif : introduction à la théorie du cerveau bayésien [The predictive mind: An introduction to Bayesian Brain Theory]. Encephale. 2022 Aug;48(4):436-444. French. doi: 10.1016/j.encep.2021.09.011. Epub 2022 Jan 7. PMID: 35012898.

[10] Danielle Cohen, "This Day in History: The 1913 Women's Suffrage Parade", The White House, https://obamawhitehouse.archives.gov/blog/2016/03/03/this-day-history-1913-womens-suffrage-parade

[11] The Jane Addams Papers Project, "NATIONAL ASSOCIATION OPPOSED TO WOMAN SUFFRAGE", The University of Illinois at Chicago, https://digital.janeaddams.ramapo.edu/items/show/15820

[12] Danielle Cohen, "This Day in History: The 1913 Women's Suffrage Parade", The White House, https://obamawhitehouse.archives.gov/blog/2016/03/03/this-day-history-1913-womens-suffrage-parade

[13] National Women's History Museum, "Alice Paul", https://www.womenshistory.org/education-resources/biographies/alice-paul

[14] Sarah Pruitt, "The Night of Terror: When Suffragists Were Imprisoned and Tortured in 1917", https://www.history.com/news/night-terror-brutality-suffragists-19th-amendment

[15] Jewish Women's Archive, "Pamphlet distributed by the National Association Opposed to Woman Suffrage", https://jwa.org/media/pamphlet-distributed-by-national-association-opposed-to-woman-suffrage

[16] National Research Council (US) and Institute of Medicine (US) Committee on Integrating the Science of Early Childhood Development; Shonkoff JP, Phillips DA, editors. From Neurons to Neighborhoods: The Science of Early Childhood Development. Washington (DC): National Academies Press (US); 2000. 8, The Developing Brain. Available from: https://www.ncbi.nlm.nih.gov/books/NBK225562/

[17] Andrew Fisher and Mark Dimmock, "Aristotelian Virtue Ethics", Open OKState, https://open.library.okstate.edu/introphilosophy/chapter/virtue-ethics/

[18] Darryl Edwards, "How to boost the happy hormones", https://www.primalplay.com/blog/play-and-the-feel-good-hormones (Accessed on Sep 2, 2023)

[19] There's a difference between hormones and neurotransmitters although it is used interchangeably nowadays. To be precise, dopamine is primarily a neurotransmitter.

[20] Salimpoor, V., Benovoy, M., Larcher, K. *et al.* Anatomically distinct dopamine release during anticipation and experience of peak emotion to

music. *Nat Neurosci* **14**, 257–262 (2011). https://doi.org/10.1038/nn.2726

[21] Colin G DeYoung, "the neuromodulator of exploration: A unifying theory of the role of dopamine in personality," Frontier, https://www.frontiersin.org/articles/10.3389/fnhum.2013.00762/full

[22] The National Registry of Exoneration, "Frank Sterling", https://www.law.umich.edu/special/exoneration/Pages/casedetail.aspx?caseid=3662

[23] The Innocence Project, "Frank Sterling", https://innocenceproject.org/cases/frank-sterling/

[24] National Registry of Exoneration, https://www.law.umich.edu/special/exoneration/Pages/about.aspx (Accessed on Oct 19, 2023)

[25] GCF Global, "Digital Media Literacy: How Filter Bubble Isolates You", https://edu.gcfglobal.org/en/digital-media-literacy/how-filter-bubbles-isolate-you/1/ (Accessed on Oct 19, 2023)

[26] Wikipedia, "Bruce Edwards Ivins",

https://en.wikipedia.org/wiki/Bruce_Edwards_Ivins?wprov=sfti1#[1]

[27] Archie Bland, "Christopher Jefferies was vilified for a murder he didn't commit - now he's a privacy crusader", Independent, https://www.independent.co.uk/news/media/press/christopher-jefferies-was-vilified-for-a-murder-he-didn-t-commit-now-he-s-a-privacy-crusader-9217643.html

---

1. https://en.wikipedia.org/wiki/Bruce_Edwards_Ivins?wprov=sfti1

28 Tracy G Lee, "The Real Story of Sunil Tripathi, the Boston Bomber Who Wasn't", NBC news, https://www.nbcnews.com/news/asian-america/wrongly-accused-boston-bombing-sunil-tripathys-story-now-being-told-n373141

29 Kendra Cherry, "What is Cognitive Dissonance?" Verywell Mind, "https://www.verywellmind.com/what-is-cognitive-dissonance-2795012"

30 Merriam-webster, "Rationalization", https://www.merriam-webster.com/dictionary/rationalization

31 Flat Earth Society, "Bedford Level Experiment", https://wiki.tfes.org/Bedford_Level_Experiment

32 Rosetta Stones, "Wallace's Woeful Wager: How a Founder of Modern Biology Got Suckered by Flat-Earthers", Scientific American, https://blogs.scientificamerican.com/rosetta-stones/wallace-8217-s-woeful-wager-how-a-founder-of-modern-biology-got-suckered-by-flat-earthers/

33 Craig A. Foster, "Do People Really Think Earth Might Be Flat?", Scientific American, https://blogs.scientificamerican.com/observations/do-people-really-think-earth-might-be-flat/

34 Steve Mirsky, "Flat Earthers: What They Believe and Why", Scientific American, https://www.scientificamerican.com/podcast/episode/flat-earthers-what-they-believe-and-why/

[35] John Uri, "Flag Day – Flying High: The Stars and Stripes in Space", NASA, https://www.nasa.gov/history/flag-day-flying-high-the-stars-and-stripes-in-space/

[36] NASA, "Blue Marble - Image of the Earth from Apollo 17", https://www.nasa.gov/image-article/blue-marble-image-of-earth-from-apollo-17/

[37] Rob Picheta, " The flat-Earth conspiracy is spreading around the globe. Does it hide a darker core?", CNN, https://edition.cnn.com/2019/11/16/us/flat-earth-conference-conspiracy-theories-scli-intl/index.html

[38] Jubilee, "Flat Earthers vs Scientists: Can We Trust Science? | Middle Ground", YouTube, https://www.youtube.com/watch?v=Q7yvvq-9ytE

[39] Boscaljon D. Beyond Literal Idolatry: Imagining Faith through Creatively Changing Identities. *Religions*. 2022; 13(9):810. https://doi.org/10.3390/rel13090810

[40] Stanford Encyclopedia of Philosophy, "Descartes' Ontological Argument", https://plato.stanford.edu/entries/descartes-ontological/

[41] Richard A. Watson, "René Descartes", Britannica, "https://www.britannica.com/biography/Rene-Descartes/Residence-in-the-Netherlands"

[42] Fred Wilson, "René Descarte, Scientific Method", Internet Encyclopedia of Philosophy, https://iep.utm.edu/rene-descartes-scientific-method/

[43] Swire-Thompson, B., Miklaucic, N., Wihbey, J., Lazer, D., & DeGutis, J. (2022). The backfire effect after correcting misinformation is strongly associated with reliability.. Journal of Experimental Psychology: General, 151(7), 1655-1665. https://doi.org/10.1037/xge0001131

[44] The Conversation US and Nir Eisikovits, "AI is an existential threat - just not the way you think", Scientific American, https://www.scientificamerican.com/article/ai-is-an-existential-threat-just-not-the-way-you-think/

[45] Dunning, D. (2011). The Dunning-Kruger effect: On being ignorant of one's own ignorance. In J. M. Olson & M. P. Zanna (Eds.), *Advances in experimental social psychology,* Vol. 44, pp. 247–296). Academic Press. https://doi.org/10.1016/B978-0-12-385522-0.00005-6[2]

[46] Kirsten Weir, "Feel like a fraud?", American Psychological Association, https://www.apa.org/gradpsych/2013/11/fraud#[3]

[47] Wikipedia, "File: Dunning–Kruger Effect 01.svg", https://en.wikipedia.org/wiki/Dunning%E2%80%93Kruger_effect

[48] ADR Times, "Positional Bargaining Explained", https://www.adrtimes.com/positional-bargaining/

[49] Harvard Law School, "What is Interest Based Negotiation?", https://www.pon.harvard.edu/tag/interest-based-negotiation/

---

2. https://psycnet.apa.org/doi/10.1016/B978-0-12-385522-0.00005-6

3. https://www.apa.org/gradpsych/2013/11/fraud

[50] Christopher Bergland, "The Neurochemicals of Happiness", Psychology Today, https://www.psychologytoday.com/us/blog/the-athletes-way/201211/the-neurochemicals-of-happiness

[51] Kim Parker and Juliana Menasce Horowitz, "Majority of workers who quit a job in 2021 cite low pay, no opportunities for advancement, feeling disrespected", Pew Research Center, https://www.pewresearch.org/short-reads/2022/03/09/majority-of-workers-who-quit-a-job-in-2021-cite-low-pay-no-opportunities-for-advancement-feeling-disrespected/

[52] Cambridge Dictionary, "Overgeneralization", https://dictionary.cambridge.org/us/dictionary/english/overgeneralization

[53] Cambridge Dictionary, "Oversimplification", https://dictionary.cambridge.org/us/dictionary/english/oversimplification

[54] Kassiani Nikolopoulou, "False Dilemma Fallacy | Examples & Definition", Scribbr, https://www.scribbr.com/fallacies/false-dilemma-fallacy/

[55] Kassiani Nikolopoulou, "What Is Straw Man Fallacy? | Definition & Examples", Scribbr, https://www.scribbr.com/fallacies/straw-man-fallacy/

[56] Lapate, R., Rokers, B., Tromp, D. *et al.* Awareness of Emotional Stimuli Determines the Behavioral Consequences of Amygdala Activation and Amygdala-Prefrontal Connectivity. *Sci Rep* 6, 25826 (2016). https://doi.org/10.1038/srep25826

[57] The Open University, "What did Plato believe about the human soul? The one minute guide", https://www.open.edu/openlearn/history-the-arts/culture/philosophy/concepts/what-did-plato-believe-about-the-human-soul-the-one-minute-guide

[58] Nathan J. Kolla, Marco Bortolato, The role of monoamine oxidase A in the neurobiology of aggressive, antisocial, and violent behavior: A tale of mice and men, Progress in Neurobiology, Volume 194, 2020, 101875, ISSN 0301-0082, https://doi.org/10.1016/j.pneurobio.2020.101875.

[59] Kimberly Holland, "Amygdala Hijack: When Emotion Takes Over", Heathline, https://www.healthline.com/health/stress/amygdala-hijack#takeaway

[60] Billman GE. Homeostasis: The Underappreciated and Far Too Often Ignored Central Organizing Principle of Physiology. Front Physiol. 2020 Mar 10;11:200. doi: 10.3389/fphys.2020.00200. PMID: 32210840; PMCID: PMC7076167.

[61] Peter Payne and Mardi A. Crane-Godreau, "The preparatory set: a novel approach to understanding stress, trauma, and the bodymind therapies", Frontiers, https://www.frontiersin.org/articles/10.3389/fnhum.2015.00178/full

[62] Medical News Today, "What is the fight, flight, or freeze response?", https://www.medicalnewstoday.com/articles/fight-flight-or-freeze-response#recovery

[63] Hudson Matt, Johnson Mark I., Perspectives on emotional memory images and the persistence of pain, Frontiers in Pain Research, Vol.4 2023, DOI 10.3389/fpain.2023.1217721, ISSN=2673-561X

[64] Liu, Y., Lin, W., Liu, C. et al. Memory consolidation reconfigures neural pathways involved in the suppression of emotional memories. Nat Commun 7, 13375 (2016). https://doi.org/10.1038/ncomms13375

[65] Friedman, N.P., Robbins, T.W. The role of prefrontal cortex in cognitive control and executive function. *Neuropsychopharmacol.* 47, 72–89 (2022). https://doi.org/10.1038/s41386-021-01132-0

[66] University of Cambridge, "Study finds that genes play a role in empathy", https://www.cam.ac.uk/research/news/study-finds-that-genes-play-a-role-in-empathy

[67] Roberto Grujičić MD, "Prefrontal cortex", https://www.kenhub.com/en/library/anatomy/prefrontal-cortex

[68] Franklin, T., Silva, B., Perova, Z. *et al.* Prefrontal cortical control of a brainstem social behavior circuit. *Nat Neurosci* 20, 260–270 (2017). https://doi.org/10.1038/nn.4470

[69] Anthony Wright, Ph.D., "Chapter 6: Limbic System: Amygdala", Neuroanatomy Online, The university of Texas McGovern Medical School, https://nba.uth.tmc.edu/neuroanatomy/

[70] Datta, D.; Arnsten, A.F.T. Loss of Prefrontal Cortical Higher Cognition with Uncontrollable Stress: Molecular Mechanisms, Changes with Age,

and Relevance to Treatment. *Brain Sci.* **2019**, *9*, 113. https://doi.org/10.3390/brainsci9050113

71 Harvard Health Publishing, "Train your brain", https://www.health.harvard.edu/mind-and-mood/train-your-brain

72 The Information Philosopher, "Libet Experiments", https://www.informationphilosopher.com/freedom/libet_experiments.html

73 Robert Sapoksy and Andrew Huberman, "Do we have free will?", YouTube, https://www.youtube.com/watch?v=RI3JCq9-bbM&t=318s

About the Author

Fiona So graduated from the University of Michigan with dual degrees in Economics and Political Science, and later pursued a Master of Business Administration at Quantic University. She now serves as a senior technical product manager in a blockchain consortium. Despite not having formal training in psychology or neuroscience, Fiona's intense curiosity and sharp observational skills have propelled her on a unique journey of understanding the human brain.

In "Shackled: Why We Are Predisposed to Resist Belief Change and How to Overcome Our Instincts," Fiona shares the culmination of years of personal exploration and research. This book is the fruit of countless hours spent reading, thinking, questioning, and engaging with complex theories, all driven by her desire to make these concepts accessible to a broad audience.

Motivated by a need to understand why change is so difficult an d ho w we ca n be tter na vigate th e ch allenges it presents, Fiona embarked on the journey of writing this book. Her hope is to empower others with insights into their own minds, enabling them to lead more mindful, intentional lives.

When not immersed in her research, Fiona enjoys honing her skills in poker and practicing the martial art of Wing Chun. She is a fervent believer in the power of lifelong learning and continuous self-improvement, a journey she is excited to share with her readers.

www.ingramcontent.com/pod-product-compliance
Lightning Source LLC
Chambersburg PA
CBHW020322290526
45785CB00007B/2880